Asylum and Immigration
A Christian Perspective on a Polarised Debate

by Nick Spencer
Jubilee Centre, Cambridge

PATERNOSTER

First published 2004 by Paternoster Press
Paternoster Press is a division of Authentic Media
9 Holdom Avenue, Bletchley, Milton Keynes, Bucks,
MK1 1QR, UK
and PO Box 1047, Waynesboro, GA 30830-2047
www.authenticmedia.co.uk/paternoster

British Library Cataloguing in Publication Data

A catalogue record for this book is available from the
British Library

ISBN 1-84227-271-3

Cover design by Sam Redwood
Print Management by Adare Carwin
Printed and bound in Denmark by AIT Nørhaven A/S

Asylum and Immigration

Contents

Acknowledgements

This book could and would not have been written without the vision and commitment of the Jubilee Centre to the idea of a Christian social vision for modern Britain.

This has its roots in the 1970s, when Michael Schluter began exploring biblical teaching in the conviction that it had a distinct, compelling and much-needed message for contemporary Britain. My thanks are owed to Michael, both for that vision and his specific comments on this manuscript.

One of the Jubilee Centre's most accomplished projects over that period has been Jonathan Burnside's study into 'the status and welfare of immigrants' in biblical law, published under that title in 2001 and much drawn on in chapters four and five of this book. My gratitude is extended to Dr Burnside for his careful research.

Less formally, but no less helpfully, John Ashcroft and Jason Fletcher have commented on several drafts of this book, and have continually offered fresh and clarifying perspectives on what I have written. Without them, the book would be a great deal less lucid than it is.

At a late stage, Arlington Trotman of the Churches' Commission for Racial Justice and Andrew Green of

MigrationwatchUK kindly read and commented on the manuscript. I have not always followed their advice but I am grateful that two people who understand this complex issue so well should offer me the benefit of their knowledge and experience. I am also grateful to Ram Gidoomal for his personal honesty and kind words of encouragement in the foreword.

I would like to register my gratitude to Paternoster for recognising the importance of and need for this book and, in particular, to Robin Parry and Lucy Atherton for their encouragement and guidance, to Helen Bannister, for her editing, and to Sam Redwood, for her excellent cover design.

Neither this book nor any other Jubilee Centre project would have happened were it not for the commitment and generosity of our supporters and donors. Having bought into the vision, they have supported it with their time, energy and money for many years. I know I speak on behalf of all the staff of the Jubilee Centre when I offer my profound gratitude for their kindness and support.

My final and greatest debt of thanks is owed to Katie, to whom this book is dedicated, who makes me feel rather less of an 'alien and stranger' here.

Nick Spencer
April 2004

Foreword

On 11 February 2004 I took part in a demonstration in London's Trafalgar Square organised by the Coalition Against the Destitution of Asylum Seekers. We were all going to spend the night sleeping rough, to highlight the injustice being done by Section 55 of the 2002 Nationality, Immigration and Asylum Act.[1] It was a symbolic protest. I can vouch for the fact that it was a bitterly cold night, and the press got some good shots of bin-liner-wrapped celebrities, but the next night I slept in my own bed again – unlike many of the estimated 10,000 asylum seekers forced into destitution by the legislation.

Why did I get involved?

In part, I wanted to make my own protest against a particularly unfair piece of legislation. A report commissioned in 2004 by the Mayor of London[2] found that 10,000 asylum seekers were being forced into destitution each year by Section 55 of the 2002 Act, because the various reasons why an individual may fail to claim asylum at his or her port of entry (such as fear, misunderstanding or a lack of legitimate documentation) were being ignored.

But I also protested because I have been an immigrant myself; I 'know how it feels to be [an] alien'.³ I arrived in Britain in the late 1960s from a conflict situation in Kenya. Stripped of possessions, assets and cultural background, I possessed only my British passport. I can well remember the atmosphere of public suspicion, fear and dislike that we East African Asians encountered, and the fact that the help of our fellow Asians already in Britain was the only effective social support that most of us had. Today, immigrants and asylum seekers are still met with fear, ignorance and suspicion, victims of Nimbyism, unwanted by many communities and often lacking support even from their own ethnic group.

As one expelled from a hostile and divided community where I experienced failed integration at first hand, I recognise that immigrants who wish to settle in a new country also have a responsibility to help create a just, stable, inclusive and cohesive society. They have an obligation, for example, to identify with their new home country, contribute to its political, economic and cultural life and not abuse the hospitality extended to them. In turn, of course, host communities have a duty to facilitate rather than frustrate such integration.

I welcome this book. I believe that Nick Spencer and the Jubilee Centre have provided an important and timely contribution to the ongoing debate.

Questions of asylum and immigration will only become more important as the new century progresses. Many believe these issues will be major battlegrounds in future general elections. The European Union is committed to a programme of immigration that will, if Britain plays her due part as a member state, bring hundreds of thousands of immigrants and asylum seekers to the UK over the next decade. This book offers a thoughtful and realistic approach to a problem that will not go away.

Fear and ignorance will persist until dispelled – a process in which this book also has a part to play. One of the most valuable sections of the book is entitled 'Slippery statistics' (chapter one), which contains some sobering illustrations of the gap between public perception of the scale of immigration and asylum in the UK and the actual, much smaller, numbers involved. Public discussion of these matters is often based on misinformation and inaccurate assumptions. This book bases its arguments securely on facts.

It is also to be welcomed because the contribution of the Christian faith is an important one. Forged in a melting pot of civilisations, propagated through minority and displaced communities, and with a global presence today, the Christian message insists on the infinite worth of every individual, however socially advantaged or disadvantaged, and maintains that communities of faith have a duty of care towards the aliens in their midst. This book's detailed study of early Israel, the Bible's teaching on immigration, and the biblical concept of nationhood make it a valuable resource for Christians and a thought-provoking analysis for people of other faiths and none. Church and State are linked in England. Why was I allowed to enter Britain in the 1960s? Partly because there was an obligation – I had a British passport – but partly because there was a principle of compassion for aliens, one that finds its roots in the Old Testament book of Leviticus.

This book's major achievement, I believe, is its persuasive transition from data and theory to principles and policy-making. You cannot, after reading these chapters, help but feel that the biblical story speaks directly and pertinently to our modern questions of asylum and immigration.

This application of faith and informed Christian thinking to social and political issues is what the Jubilee

Centre exists to promote. Throughout its twenty years, it has placed particular emphasis on right relationships as the central theme of biblical ethical teaching. As it has long argued, public policy should begin with a concern for relationships and seek to create an environment that nurtures rather than undermines them. Right relationships, rather than wealth, freedom or even equality is the 'big idea' that should guide our thinking about the social order.

In the immigration and asylum debate, the biblical concern for relationships insists on society's duty to 'love the alien' in practical and meaningful ways. In Old Testament Israel immigrants were repeatedly classed among the most vulnerable members of society and, as such, were a central concern of the law. But the biblical concern for relationships also places real value on the integrity and cohesion of communities: shared values matter. People who settle in a new country need to know, respect and value the host culture, just as that society needs to fulfil its responsibilities to its newest and often most vulnerable members.

I have been involved with the Jubilee Centre and its sister charities in several ways over the years, for example as Chair of the Steering Committee of the City and East London Employment Bond. So although it is a pleasure, it is no surprise to find in this short book the expected mastery of research, a relational and people-focused analysis, and a realistic yet challenging combination of biblical principles with the practicalities of economics, politics and that hard-to-quantify phenomenon, British society, in all its rich diversity.

Ram Gidoomal, CBE

1. 'Whatever You Say, Say Nothing'

Introduction

Writing about asylum and immigration is rather like walking on ice. The subject is lethally slippery, the ground beneath your feet of uncertain strength and the writer never quite sure that a single, misplaced phrase will not send him crashing into the freezing waters of public opprobrium. Referring to people's inability to talk honestly about the bloodshed in 1970s Northern Ireland, Seamus Heaney once wrote:

> The times are out of joint …
> … to be saved you must only save face
> And whatever you say, you say nothing.[1]

It is tempting to appropriate these lines for the closely linked topics of asylum and immigration. It is dangerous to suggest that asylum and immigration should be limited or that the historic British identity be preserved for fear of being labelled small minded or crypto-racist. It is equally dangerous to suggest that asylum and immigration should be actively encouraged or that a new

British identity forged for fear of being labelled a soft touch or a bleeding-heart liberal. To be on the safe side and save face, whatever you say, you should say nothing.

Understanding this anxiety not only helps us circumvent the tone of polemic and hysteria which so often mars the debate, and so say something constructive, but also grasp many of the factors which make the issue so very important.

No discussion of immigration can begin without acknowledging the spectre of racism that casts its long shadow across the whole debate. The twentieth century's legacy of unprecedented and unimaginable genocide, motivated by ethnic rivalry or justified by social Darwinism, will remain with the human race for millennia. On a smaller but hardly less important scale, post-war immigration to Britain exposed a latent racism in many Britons, with Afro-Caribbean, Pakistani and Bangladeshi immigrants enduring the same prejudice that earlier Irish immigrants had suffered, only intensified by their different skin colour. From the riots in Nottingham and North Kensington in 1958 to the murder of Stephen Lawrence in 1993, post-war Britain has numerous milestones marking its painful history of race relations.[2]

More alarmingly, recent years have seen the far right gaining ground in continental Europe. Jorg Haider's Freedom Party won 27 per cent of the vote in the 1999 Austrian elections and Jean-Marie Le Pen's National Front polled six million votes to beat socialist Prime Minster Lionel Jospin into second place in the 2001 French general elections. In Denmark, the Danish People's Party is currently the country's third largest party. In Italy, the Northern League and National Alliance parties entered a coalition government with Silvio Berlusconi following the 2001 elections. In

Switzerland, the Swiss People's Party ran newspaper advertisements blaming crime on 'black Africans' before capturing 27 per cent of the vote in the 2003 elections. In the Netherlands, the assassinated Pym Fortuyn's LPF recently came second behind the centre-right Christian Democrat Party. In comparison, the British National Party is an insignificant affair, although its success in recent local elections made it newsworthy. These far right parties are by no means unanimous in their policies but are united in their determined and often aggressive anti-immigration stance.

The insignificance of the British National Party has not prevented the phrase 'institutionally racist' from being thrown about with careless abandon. Defined and popularised by the MacPherson enquiry into the death of Stephen Lawrence as 'the collective failure of an organisation to provide an appropriate and professional service to people because of their colour, culture or ethnic origin', it has become the phrase of choice for confessions and accusations alike.

In the wake of the MacPherson enquiry, the head of the prison service asserted that the service was 'institutionally racist'. At a press conference to launch its report *Raising the Attainment of Minority Ethnic Pupils*, inspectors from The Office for Standards in Education claimed that many of Britain's schools were 'institutionally racist'.[3] In a interview in June 2002, the Director of Public Prosecutions, countering suggestions that the Crown Prosecution Service was racist, claimed that 'British society is institutionally racist … the whole of society has a problem.'[4]

The popularity of the phrase and the eagerness with which it has been used over recent years is both unnerving and unhelpful. In much the same way as the people of Salem, in their determination to destroy witchcraft, found themselves haunted by it at every juncture, so our eagerness to eradicate racism is in danger of having the same effect, inducing paranoia and a spate of accusations and confessions, and making any more balanced and nuanced analysis very difficult.

A matter of life and death

Another reason for our anxiety is that, perhaps more than any other contemporary issue, it really matters. Education, transport and social security are all important domestic issues but unlike asylum they are rarely matters of life and death.

Many of the people who end up on British soil claiming asylum do so because they would be dead had they remained where they were. The most common provenances of British asylum applicants between 2001 and 2003 – Afghanistan, Iraq and Somalia – speak for themselves: all are areas of major political and military instability.[5] According to a report published by the Institute for Public Policy Research in May 2003, repression, discrimination, ethnic conflict, human rights abuses, and civil war were the most common reasons for forced migration into the EU in the 1990s.[6]

Reaching British soil is, in itself, no guarantee of safety. On 19 June 2000, 60 Chinese immigrants were found in Dover in the back of the container lorry that was smuggling them into Britain. Fifty eight had suffocated to death. A year later Firsat Dag, a young man who had fled Turkey for taking part in a pro-Kurdish demonstration, was stabbed to death in the Sighthill area of Glasgow. Whilst all political issues deal with important subjects, few are quite so immersed in matters of life and death. It is hardly surprising that the debate is so highly charged.

A matter of identity

Beyond the violence and humanitarian crises that underpin many claims of asylum, there is the less shocking but hardly less motivating issue of personal and national identity. Again, unlike other major areas of policy, asylum and immigration force both immigrants and host nations to ask of themselves the one question which marks us out as human: who am I?

The answer to that question incorporates a vast range of factors. Ethnicity, religion, family, language, cultural praxis, education, social mores, and personal history will all contribute to an individual's answer, and a nation's response will include many of these whilst adding national history, political system, social structure, and implicit cultural values.

When an individual migrates across national boundaries, either by choice or necessity, many of these fundamental elements come into sharp focus and attain particular importance. When mass migration occurs the same thing happens not only to the migrant group but also to the nation in which it settles. A number of intractable questions are posed, the most basic of which is 'which identity, if either, prevails when two alternatives meet?'

In reality, the question is almost always rather more subtle and involves the gradual mutation of the various factors which comprise *both* identities. Yet, this does little to lessen its importance. Even when asylum and immigration is not a matter of life and death, it is often one of dignity and humanity. What is at stake, in our language, culture and values, is what makes us human.

Clarifying terms

Much of our difficulty in talking fruitfully about asylum and immigration is due to our confusion and abuse of relevant terms. Without a cogent, coherent and comprehensible vocabulary no genuine or effective debate is possible.

Technically, the variety of terms available should facilitate the debate. Yet, our tendency to nuance, load or completely misuse them often confuses the argument. 'Political migrant', 'economic migrant', 'immigrant', 'illegal immigrant', 'asylum seeker', 'family settler', 'alien', and 'refugee' are often used interchangeably and even confused with altogether different concepts such as ethnicity or religion. Such confusion makes constructive debate almost impossible. Even the (deliberate) use of the dual phrase 'asylum and immigration' in paragraphs above can be problematic. The two entities are linked but distinct, and pairing them together can often serve to blur important differences.

Popular confusion is not helped by internal differences. One Home Office report remarks, 'sources of data which shed light on stocks and flows of migrants use widely differing concepts and definitions,' before going on to examine the varying definitions of 'migrants', 'foreign workers' and 'foreign-born workers' in the International Passenger Survey, the Labour Force Survey and the National Census.[7] 'It is crucial,' it concludes, 'to understand the concepts and definitions involved.'

It is, indeed, crucial but that does it make it easy. The Oxford English Dictionary definition of an immigrant is 'one who settles as a permanent resident in a different country'[8] but this is somewhat narrower than that used in government reports. One such report says:

migrants are defined as all those who were born outside the UK – a group which makes up eight per cent of the total UK population, or almost ten per cent of the working age population (some 4.8 million people in total including 3.6 million people of working age.)[9]

This definition, as the huge numbers suggest, allows for a heterogeneous group. Some immigrants, as the report explains, have been living in the UK for decades. Approximately 47 per cent have acquired British citizenship. Others, almost a third of the total immigrant population in fact, have arrived during the last decade. The term 'immigrant', therefore, can incorporate those who have lived in Britain for a week and those who have lived there for 50 years. It includes those who have come as refugees, as students, for reasons of family reunion, and as part of the highly-skilled migrant programme. A more precise definition of immigrant is the one used in the International Passenger Survey, the government's continuous, voluntary sample survey of all international passengers, but this precision is often lost in popular debate.[10]

Research has shown that 'migrant experiences are more polarised than those for the population as a whole with larger concentrations at the extremes (e.g. of wealth and poverty, high and low skills).'[11] It is not too much of an exaggeration to say that immigrants can differ at least as much from each other as they do from the general population.[12] This is recognised all too infrequently, with people using the terms 'migrant' or 'immigrant' as if they were exact and precise tools rather than the blunt instruments they are bound to be.

Asylum seekers are, by nature, a more homogeneous group, but even this term is misused, often being confused with the term refugee. The official definition of a refugee derives from the 1951 United Nations Convention relating to the Status of Refugees, extended in its application by the 1967 Protocol relating to the Status of Refugees, to which the UK is a signatory. This defines a refugee as a person who:

> owing to a well-founded fear of being persecuted for reasons of race, religion, nationality, membership of a particular social group or political opinion, is outside the country of his nationality and unable or, owing to such fear, is unwilling to avail himself of the protection of that country; or who, not having a nationality and being outside the country of his former habitual residence ... is unable or, owing to such fear, is unwilling to return to it...[13]

Even this definition is narrow, however, as it excludes people fleeing for reasons of war and famine, as opposed to persecution, as well as those who are persecuted but remain refugees in their own country. As one report remarks, 'the majority of forced migrants move for reasons not recognised by the international refugee regime ... many are displaced within their own country of origin.'[14] The United Nations High Commissioner for Refugees estimates that there are around 6 million Internally Displaced Persons (IDPs) who do not count as refugees.[15] The total global refugee population includes 'convention' and 'non-convention' refugees, as well as Internally Displaced Persons.

An asylum seeker, on the other hand, is 'someone who has fled their country of origin in order to make an asylum claim in another country.'[16] He or she is someone 'whose claims for refugee status have not yet been decided.'[17] These subtleties are sometimes lost in the debate. Not only are 'asylum seekers' clearly different from 'immigrants' (although they are, by definition, immigrants), but they are also different from 'refugees' by dint of having made a specific claim. Technically speaking (although the reality is rather different) an individual can only be an asylum seeker for a limited period of time, until their case has been decided one way or another. People can spend entire lifetimes as refugees.

Unfortunately, recognising the drawbacks in terminology and using the lexicon as precisely as possible is no guarantee of a rational debate. Words and phrases are invariably susceptible to manipulation, irrespective of how carefully they are used, and this is particularly the case when dealing with new policy initiatives. How one feels about the idea of detaining asylum seekers until their claims are decided will be subtly influenced by whether they are held in 'detention centres', 'accommodation centres' or 'welcome centres'. In much the same way as some seasoned journalists eschew the term 'terrorist', recognising it as a word which prejudges a situation, so anyone who voices an opinion on asylum and immigration is caught in a Catch 22 of saying too much by saying anything. Whatever you say, your audience will second-guess your opinions.

There is, in reality, little that can be done about this except for maintaining a vigilant approach to terms used. At the very least, such an attitude will steer you away from the many 'trigger' terms that cross the debate like trip wires. 'Flooded', 'soft touch', 'bogus', 'scrounger', 'refugee magnet', and 'racist' are just a handful of those phrases invaluable to those who wish to write polemic but ruinous to those who wish to say anything constructive.

Slippery statistics

If it were simply a case of clarifying and avoiding certain terms, discussing asylum and immigration would be a reasonably straightforward issue. However, there is a bigger obstacle to constructive debate. The facts themselves are nothing like as self-evident as we sometimes think.

This is partly reflected in the fact that virtually every organisation which ventures into this arena boasts some kind of 'get the real facts here' section.[18] Quite understandably, relevant bodies are concerned to counter popular misunderstanding and misinformation, of which there is a great deal.

When MORI asked people in June 2002 what percentage of the world's refugees they thought the UK hosted, the average answer was 23 per cent, several times higher than the correct answer.[19] The following year, another survey asked what percentage of the British population people thought were immigrants to the country, giving immigrant a broad definition, '(i.e. not born in the UK)'. Fewer than 1 in 10 respondents knew the right answer and the average response was 21 per cent, around three times higher than the true figure.[20]

The same survey showed that, although 50 per cent of people thought that asylum seekers came to Britain 'because they have been persecuted in their countries', 45 per cent said it was 'because they want to live off social security payments,' and 64 per cent thought it was 'because they think Britain is a "soft touch"'. In reality, as far as it is possible to tell, there is 'very little evidence' that asylum seekers have 'a detailed knowledge of UK immigration or asylum procedures; entitlements to benefits in the UK; or the availability of work in the UK.' Moreover, there is 'even less evidence that [they have] ... a comparative knowledge of how these phenomena varied between different European countries.'[21] Similar confusion exists over the amount asylum seekers receive in benefit. One survey reported that the public believes asylum seekers receive £113 a week in benefits, whereas the true figure is around £37.[22]

Such misinformation is more serious than it may first appear, as it is upon such questionable 'facts' that erroneous and sometime malign assumptions are built. One recent survey reported that young people's views of asylum seekers and refugees were largely negative, with only one in five 15- to 24-year olds agreeing that 'asylum seekers and refugees make a positive contribution to life in this country', and nearly three in five disagreeing (20 per cent 'neither agreed nor disagreed').[23] When inaccurate statistics are used to construct arguments that carelessly denounce or demonise whole groups of people, let alone people who are already vulnerable, rectifying them becomes extremely important.

The misinformation works in both directions, however. The common assumption that 'Britain is a nation of immigrants' is, at best, meaningless and, at worst, simply wrong. Britain is a nation of immigrants only inasmuch as every nation is. In actual fact, except for the arrival of 100,000 Huguenots from France in the seventeenth century, and a similar number of Jews in the nineteenth century and again in early the twentieth century, Britain experienced no numerically significant migration in the 850 years before 1950.[24]

In a different area, cases of HIV, TB and Hepatitis B have increased considerably in Britain over the last decade or so, and much of this increase is due to immigration. There is also good anecdotal evidence that 'the NHS is being drained of millions of pounds a year by overseas visitors receiving "free" medical treatment to which they are not entitled.'[25] Simply because 'NHS tourism' is a term bandied about by scaremongering sections of the media, it does not mean it isn't true.

In the same way as cleaning our language is not as simple as we would like it to be, clarifying our statistics is a difficult business. Whilst some facts quoted above can be easily corrected, others are vulnerable to subjective definitions, inexact estimates and straight-forward ignorance.

One's attitude to the number of refugees a nation should host will vary according to whether one is thinking about the total refugee population, the refugee population per 1,000 inhabitants, the refugee population per square mile, or the refugee population per US\$1m GDP. Each is a valid metric, each gives a different picture of which nation bears the heaviest 'burden' of refugees and each will have implications on which nation should accommodate more refugees.[26]

Similarly, one's attitude to the economic benefits of immigration to a host nation will depend on whether one considers the effect of immigration on GDP or its effect on GDP per capita. Again, each metric is valid and each can give a different answer. It also, incidentally, depends on viewing 'immigrants' as a natural, homogenous group which, as we have seen, is a questionable assumption.

Over and above these varying measurements, there is the basic fact that the 'facts' are not always known. Many arguments are based on forecasts which, given the variety of extenuating circumstances, cannot be truly reliable. If resident population estimates can be inaccurate (witness the confusion over the actual population size following the 2001 National Census), immigration forecasts will almost inevitably be so. One of the most contentious elements in the whole debate, the number of illegal immigrants present in a nation, is, almost by definition, completely unknown.

Because the scale and nature of both asylum in and immigration to the UK is a relatively modern phenomenon, and because the issues which arise from them never 'settle' but change and modify over generations, the necessary data are often simply not available. Home Office studies are littered with the urgent calls for more work to be done.[27] Ultimately, no matter how good one's intentions are to form a rational, balanced, nuanced opinion, if the information isn't there, it can't be done. In the words of the Institute for Public Policy Research, 'the availability and quality of data in this area makes it extremely difficult to provide the empirical information and analysis needed for evidence based policy.'[28]

Trying to say something

Recognising the sensitivity of the debates that surround asylum and immigration and our difficulty in talking about the issues involved, without descending into paranoid anxiety or ill-tempered polemic, is not simply an academic exercise. Instead, by locating and helping us understand the various mines which litter the landscape, it enables us to avoid them and, hopefully, therefore, to make a constructive contribution to the debate.

It reminds us that rather than simply discussing 'policy', we are dealing with people's lives, security, relationships and identity, and that at all times we need to maintain a tone of sensitively, respect and humanity. It reminds us that we need to use words as carefully as we can, to eschew inflammatory language and trigger phrases, and to be as precise with terminology as possible, but also to recognise that mistakes are easily made and that embarking on witch hunts against those whom we deem to have spoken inappropriately is counterproductive. It reminds us that we need to be as honest and exact with statistics as possible, and to maintain the humility which recognises that, with the best will in the world, we may be wrong. Any genuinely Christian response to asylum and immigration in Britain today should begin with these caveats.

This analysis is written with these points in mind and it is hoped that it will, accordingly, add something to a debate that seems to be one of the defining issues of our time.

2. Issues of Asylum

Setting the Scene

Asylum is one of the most important issues facing Western governments today. Politicians like to talk tough about it. Newspapers run campaigns on it. Far right parties capitalise on people's fear and loathing. The general public in the UK rates it (coupled with its close cousin, immigration) behind only the National Health Service as the most important issue facing Britain today.[1]

This chapter sets the scene for a Christian analysis of asylum by examining the facts and figures, both from the UK and more broadly, on which various claims are based and by assessing the reasons behind the rise in asylum applications. It then moves on to examine the contours of the contemporary debate, touching on issues such as legality, justice, mercy and humanity, before concluding with a look at the fundamental principles that underpin the entire debate.

Asylum: facts and figures

'We are seeing real signs of improvement right across the asylum system.' So spoke David Blunkett after a dramatic fall in asylum applications in the first quarter of 2003 was announced. Between January and March that year 16,000 people applied for asylum in the UK, a fall of over 7,000 on the previous quarter, and the figure for the whole year was 41 per cent less than that of 2002.[2]

The reasons for the fall, the Home Secretary explained, could be found in the reforms introduced in the Nationality, Immigration and Asylum Act the previous November. These included restricting access to benefits for those who did not claim early, a clampdown on 'benefit shopping' in the EU, measures to tackle 'pull factors' such as the capacity to work illegally, measures to 'simplify the appeals process', and the inclusion of ten countries on the 'white list' (a list of countries to which refused asylum applicants could be removed quickly and without right of appeal). These changes, combined with others such as measures to secure the Channel Tunnel, moving UK border controls to France, the creation of a system of accommodation centres for asylum seekers, and the determined tackling of people-trafficking, were responsible for the unprecedented fall in figures.

The following day, May 23 2003, the newspapers reacted with a mixture of irritation and incredulity. 'Playing this crude numbers games plays into the hands of xenophobes', began *The Independent* editorial, after having given over its entire front page (subtitled 'why you shouldn't believe everything you are told by the Government, the Tories and the right-wing press') to asylum statistics.[3] 'Facts behind the figures are not so encouraging,' ran the title of the analysis in *The Daily Telegraph*, after having dedicated a title and a cartoon to the issue on its front page. 'Doubts over Blair asylum "triumph",' read the *Daily Mail* headline, on pages six and seven.

In spite of their different responses, most newspapers agreed that the fall in figures was something of a fait accompli given that the previous quarter had witnessed the highest figures on record. As *The Independent* put it, when 'Tony Blair made his surprise pledge to halve the number of asylum-seekers in a year ... he had loaded the dice in his favour by choosing what he knew was a record baseline.'

This 'record baseline' was 8,900 applications in October 2002, which contributed to a record 23,385 in the fourth quarter of the year, which made up the record of 85,865 for 2002.[4] This figure was a 20 per cent increase on the 2001 total of 71,700[5] and a 7 per cent increase on the previous record high of 80,315 in 2000.[6] These figures compare sharply with the average for 1991–98 of around 35,000 applications per year, and of around 4,000 per annum in the mid-1980s.[7] All figures exclude dependants. Asylum is rated a highly important issue by the British public for the simple reason that recent years have witnessed unprecedented numbers of people claiming asylum.

The UK is by no means alone in having to deal with these exceptionally high rates, however. According to the UNHCR, the current global 'convention refugee' population is around 11 million, down from a high of 18 million in the immediate post-Cold War period, but considerably more than the estimated 9 million in 1980 or 2.5 million in 1975.[8] Pakistan and Iran between them host nearly a third of all refugees, the majority of them coming from Afghanistan, but in terms of refugee population per 1,000 inhabitants or per US$1m GDP Armenia and Guinea bear considerably heavier burdens.[9] Whichever measurement one uses, the one undeniable fact is that the vast majority of refugees live in low-income countries.

Asylum applicants are, as already mentioned, different to refugees by the fact of their application and this is reflected in the data. UNHCR estimates that there are currently about one million asylum applicants in the world and that of the 50 or so industrialised nations which account for around two-thirds of these applications, the UK received most between 2001 and 2003.[10]

According to applications received per 1,000 population, however, the UK came eleventh, both for the period 1992–2001 and for the more recent period of increased applications, 2001–2003, with 0.97 applications per 1,000 inhabitants in the 90s and 1.44 per 1,000 in the more recent period. Over the 1990s Switzerland was ranked highest with nearly 4 applications per 1,000 inhabitants per year and in recent years Switzerland, Sweden, Luxembourg, Norway, Austria, and Ireland have all returned figures of over 2 applicants per 1,000 population per year.

By a third measure, applications received per US$1m GDP, the UK came forth-eighth globally and twelfth in the list of industrialised nations behind – among other Western European nations – Belgium, Austria, the Netherlands, Ireland and Switzerland.

Statistics and rankings can obscure the details and subtleties of a complex situation (not to mention reduce human beings to numbers) and so need to be treated with some care. Nevertheless, in this instance the data show that refugees and asylum applicants are a thoroughly international phenomenon and although the unprecedented number of claims that the UK has faced over recent years is comparatively high, the challenges that they present to the country are by no means unique.

Asylum: reasons behind the figures*

When examining the reasons behind the recent world-wide upsurge in asylum applications, it soon becomes clear that one is operating in a quagmire of complex, vague or non-existent information.

Broadly speaking there are three elements to the asylum process: leaving a country, travelling to a (potential) host notion, and claiming asylum in it. Each of these factors will necessarily influence the overall picture, but research suggests that it is the first of these, the so-called 'push factors', which is most important.

A study of the causes and patterns of forced migration to the EU between 1990 and 2000 conducted by the Institute for Public Policy Research (IPPR) showed that 20 countries accounted for 77 per cent of all asylum applications over this period. The research identified eight potential 'push factors' among these countries.

1. Repression and/or discrimination of minorities, ethnic conflict and human rights abuse
2. Civil war
3. Number of IDPs (internally displaced persons) to total population
4. Poverty
5. Position on the HDI (Human Development Index)
6. Life expectancy
7. Population density
8. Adult illiteracy rate

Of the ten countries from which the majority of EU asylum applicants originated, all ten exhibited the first

* This section draws in particular on *States of Conflict: Causes and patterns of forced migration to the EU and policy responses* by Stephen Castles, Heaven Crawley and Sean Loughna (London: IPPR, 2003)

'push factor', seven the second and six the third, whereas only three had life expectancy as a factor and only one had population density. [11]

This prevelance of push factors motivating EU asylum applications was echoed in a 2002 Home Office Study of UK asylum applications, *Understanding the decision-making of asylum seekers*.[12] The research was based on a literature review and on qualitative interviews with 65 asylum applicants and found that, 'the principal aim of respondents in the sample was to reach a place of safety.' Such qualitative findings chime with the statistical evidence for the UK. In 2002, the top five applicant nationalities were Iraq (17 per cent), Zimbabwe (9 per cent), Afghanistan (9 per cent), Somalia (8 per cent) and China (4 per cent).[13] The previous year they had been Afghanistan (13 per cent), Iraq (9 per cent), Somalia (9 per cent), Sri Lanka (8 per cent) and Turkey (5 per cent).[14] Such provenances can leave little doubt about the role of conflict and oppression in the motivation of asylum applicants.

A similar conclusion was reached by Churches Together in Britain and Ireland, who interviewed 146 people from 37 countries for their report *Asylum Voices*.[15] This found that very often 'decisions were not calculated or even rational', and that 'almost invariably' what drove people to leave their home countries was 'fear' based on ethnic, religious, political or gender-motivated persecution.

It should be clear from these studies, not to mention other, more anecdotal evidence that asylum application is motivated heavily by 'push factors'. Quite apart from anything else, this makes intuitive sense. As one 17-year-old Afghani woman said in the *Asylum Voices* research, 'no one would like to leave their lifelong friends.'

However, it is important to recognise that such studies, whilst credible and important, have their problems. Interviewee samples are, by their very nature, self-selecting. Those asylum seekers who are resident without legal warrant tend not to volunteer themselves for research surveys. As one Home Office report has said, 'the experiences of those in the sample group do not necessarily correspond with the wider population of asylum seekers. It may be that those who are genuinely in need of protection are more willing to engage in research of this kind.'[16]

Given that it is impossible to estimate the size, let alone the nature, of this invisible category, it is extremely hazardous to draw conclusions from it. However, it is equally dangerous to assume that because existing studies do not account for these people, they do not exist. The story told by *Asylum Voices* and the others, may be the truth but it is almost certainly not the whole truth.

In any case, research does confirm the importance of other factors. Given the nature of the overall process of seeking asylum and the fact that there has been no direct correlation between the number of refugees and the number of asylum applicants worldwide over the last 20 years, one would expect this.[17]

The research for IPPR reported that there was quite a range of potential 'pull factors' for the EU, including 'a high level of peace and public order', 'democratic institutions and the rule of law', 'economic factors' and 'welfare and health systems'.[18] Beyond these, there are also issues such as geographic proximity, historical and cultural links, post-colonial connections, a common language, and the existence of displaced communities, all of which act as 'selection factors', causing potential asylum applicants to prioritise one destination over another.

Home Office research specific to the UK records similar factors. Among the key 'pull factors' are 'the presence of relatives or friends', '[the] belief that the UK is a safe, tolerant and democratic country', 'previous links between [the asylum seeker's] own country and the UK including colonialism', and '[the] ability to speak English'. Further evidence, such as that offered by the Centre for Policy Studies report *No System to Abuse*, suggests that the potential for free healthcare is also a genuine pull factor.[19]

Talk of 'pull factors' can make people nervous, as it can caricature asylum seekers as 'scroungers'. It should, therefore, be (re-)emphasised that most research projects concur that, 'there [is] little evidence that [asylum seekers] had detailed knowledge of UK immigration or asylum procedures, entitlements to benefits in the UK, or the availability of work in the UK ... [and] even less evidence that [they] knew how such features compared with other European countries,' prior to their application.[20] At the same time, it is important not to ignore evidence or paint an incomplete picture simply because some data may be used implicitly to dehumanise asylum applicants.

The final factor in the asylum trend is in the process of transportation. The ease with which an individual is able to travel from their home country or their first port-of-call to the country in which they finally claim asylum will inevitably influence the numbers of applications any nation receives.

Unfortunately, because so much trafficking is invisible, analysis is very difficult. As far as it is possible to tell, the trends in the 1990s towards cheaper and better communication, easier and cheaper transportation, and a large 'pool' of refugees on which traffickers can draw, have encouraged people trafficking. Yet, it remains not only an extraordinarily expensive venture but, as the death of 58 Chinese men and women in the back of the container lorry in Dover in 2000 illustrates, a dangerous one too.

The Home Office report already quoted cites the 'ability to pay for long distance travel' as one of the factors influencing asylum applicants, and reports that 'some asylum seekers had to be satisfied with intermediate destinations including, in some cases, the UK.' It also claims that 'agents played a key role in channelling the asylum seekers to particular countries [with] some ... facilitating travel to a destination chosen by the asylum seeker [and] some asylum seekers [having] no choice and [being] sent to particular countries by their agent. Other agents offered asylum seekers a priced "menu" of destinations to choose from.' Such variety reminds us of the complexity of this factor.

Overall, therefore, the main driver behind the consistently high, although relatively static number of asylum applications to the EU and other industrialised nations over the last ten years is undoubtedly the instability, poverty and viciousness of certain countries and their regimes. This must also lie behind the UK asylum application story, although the fact that applications to the UK tripled in the 1990s whereas those to the EU rose by only 2 per cent and those to North America by 9 per cent powerfully suggests that 'pull' and 'transport' factors do play an important role.[21]

Whilst there is little evidence to suggest that 'pull' factors outplay 'push' ones in an individual's decision making, it is likely that people's exact destination will be influenced by ease and cost of transport, and the perceived merits of different potential destinations. Indeed, if this were not the case, no government policy would make any difference to the number of asylum claims, which clearly is not the case, and, accordingly, nobody would care about government policy, which is equally obviously untrue.

Contours of the debate

These, then, are the factual foundations of the debate. Public concern reflects an unprecedented increase in asylum applications over recent years, both to industrialised nations in general and to the UK in particular. Asylum is unquestionably driven by 'push' factors, such as persecution, discrimination, war and poverty, but it is shaped and directed by other elements, including historic ties, perceptions of different destinations and the motives of international people traffickers.

Understanding these foundations is only the first step towards grasping the contours of the contemporary debate, however, the outline of which may be seen in two types of image.

The first is the 'Sangatte' image. It is dark, hazy footage, taken at night, and ominously unclear. In it numberless young men, perhaps hundreds, apparently fit, well-fed and clothed, leave the Red Cross camp and run into the darkness. They dodge security lights and cameras, scale the Channel Tunnel perimeter fence and venture into the blackness. It is also the image of dozens of corpses being removed from a container lorry at Dover, of people traffickers driving BMWs or of asylum seekers carrying mobile phones and wearing branded trainers. It is the visual embodiment of the word 'bogus', the picture behind such headlines as 'Stop this Asylum Madness Now' (*The Sun*, 18 August 2003) and such conclusions as 'There is a timebomb ticking in our midst which must be defused' (*The Sun*, 19 August 2003). It symbolises the reasonable, if sometimes hysterical, fear of a nation which feels it has lost control of its borders, and is being exploited by the ruthless and dishonest.

The second image is of black clothed mourners at the funeral of Firsat Dag, the 22-year-old Kurdish asylum applicant, killed in Glasgow in August 2001, whose death was the first of any asylum applicant to come to national prominence and led to a rethink of asylum settlement in that city. It is the sight of the all-but-slum accommodation that many successful asylum applicants live in. It is the memory of Mohammed Isa Hasan Ali, another 22-year old, who was attacked and killed in February 2003 in Southampton city centre, having arrived in the UK after losing an eye and suffering permanent back scarring from being tortured by the Taliban. It symbolises the disgust which many feel with the use of the word 'bogus' and the nervousness they have when the natural metaphor of 'flow' (as in 'inflow' and 'outflow') is extended to 'tides', 'floods' and 'swamps'. It is the image behind many attempts to debunk the 'myth' of traditional British hospitality and tolerance. It symbolises the reasonable, if sometimes self-righteous, anger at the maltreatment of vulnerable human beings by a supposedly civilised nation.

These two positions represent the main concerns that the UK has with the issue of asylum today, and also the tension that runs through the debate. On the one hand, there is the question of legality and justice. Does the UK have control of its borders? Are people cheating the system, and, if so, what can be done about it? On the other hand, there is the question of humanity and mercy. Is the UK treating innocent and vulnerable people with appropriate humanity? If not, why not and what can be done about it?

These are the issues to which we turn now, before examining the question of values and principles that ultimately underpin both.

Justice and legality: controlling the borders

On 23 July 2003, as part of their Asylum Day, BBC1 broadcast a Panorama special entitled 'The asylum game'. In it a BBC reporter (who had been a genuine asylum applicant herself a number years previously) posed as Mihaela Cornea, a Moldovan national fleeing her violent boyfriend. She turned up at a Channel port police station and claimed asylum. Although her case was unconvincing and the authorities were clearly suspicious, she still received papers which enabled her to stay for six months. Within hours they had lost track of her.

The programme then explored the dilemma she faced. Whilst waiting for her asylum application that would take months to process, she was not allowed to work. Without benefits or accommodation she was forced into the world of illegal employment, where she obtained false documents, worked as a hotel cleaner, became involved with criminal gangs, and finally made a second, fraudulent claim when her six months permission to stay ran out and her original application was denied. Even after having been fingerprinted on her first application, her second, false claim was not immediately detected.

Along the way she met harassed, inept but well-meaning officials, selfless volunteers, criminal gangs (some of whom had made a fortune by exploiting the system), genuine applicants nervously caught in this limbo world, corrupt immigration lawyers, employers who turned a blind eye to her status (and some who didn't), and at the end some extremely angry immigration officials. The overall impression was of a system without order, method or fairness, a system that was little more than a 'chaotic shambles'.

Not surprisingly, the programme drew a hostile response from the Home Secretary the following day. John Ware, the programme's presenter, had 'plumbed new depths for what used to be television's flagship current affairs programme.' He had 'argued that the fact that asylum seekers can appeal against a refusal of their claims stops anyone from being detained and removed, which is completely false.' He had made 'unsubstantiated claim[s]' that 'all the projected population growth in the next 20 years will come from migration' and that 'two million extra houses will be needed' over the same period. Most importantly, he failed to admit that 'the undercover journalist posing as an asylum seeker … was detected by the immigration authorities … [after the] new fingerprinting system showed up a match [between her two applications]. She was told that she was about to be detained and removed from the country, at which point she owned up to being a journalist.'[22]

Blunkett's response may have corrected some of the more tendentious aspects of the BBC programme but it did little to change the impression of a system that simply did not work. It was all too easy for the reporter to slip into the anonymous, shadowy underworld of pending and failed applicants. The fingerprinting system may have detected her in the end but the intervening six months was a failure by anyone's standards. For the fraudulent applicant it gave undeserved leeway; for the genuine applicant it compounded woes; for the unscrupulous employer it offered cheap labour; and for criminal gangs it provided ample opportunity to make money from people's desperation and society's vulnerability.

The true extent of these failures and the number of people who exist in semi-legal limbo is unknown and unknowable. Of the total initial decisions made in 2002, around 34 per cent of asylum applications were granted, and this fell to 17 per cent in 2003. Yet, over the same period, asylum removals, including voluntary departures, rose to 10,740 (itself a record figure) in 2002 and then to 12,490 in 2003.[23] Estimates suggest that the Home Office loses touch with thousands of failed asylum applicants each year and that on average only around a quarter of failed seekers are eventually removed.

The reasons for the low removal rate are various. Many countries do not want to take back failed asylum applicants mainly because their economies benefit from the revenue that asylum applicants (and illegal workers) send back to their country of origin.

Removal orders can be difficult or impossible to enforce, sometimes because the failed asylum applicant has no papers, sometimes because the embassy does not accept that the applicant comes from its country, and sometimes because the country's national government is such that effective removal procedures are impossible to organise.

Until recently, most refused asylum applicants could lodge an appeal against the decision to remove them, during which time they were free to stay at an agreed address and required to report to a police station or immigration officer at regular intervals. This system appears to have been inadequately resourced, however, and a significant number of asylum applicants did not abide by the conditions and could not easily be traced. The plurality of national communities, especially in London, made the evasion and integration of failed applicants relatively straightforward. As Keith Best, head of the Immigration Advisory Service, told MPs in

June 2003, Britain's diverse population makes it easier for immigrants simply to 'disappear'.

Such abuse of the asylum system is closely linked, at least in the public's mind, to the issue of illegal immigration. There is evidence that many individuals enter the country illegally and work without permit and only claim asylum if and when they are discovered. Still others overstay on a visitor's visa, give false information in order to gain permission to enter the UK, or are in possession of false documents and, once again, only claim asylum once their misdemeanours have been discovered.

Estimates of illegal workers are usually put between several hundred thousand and one million, with the majority being employed in the UK's unregulated economy, particularly in catering, construction, clothes manufacturing, agriculture and the sex industry. There is some concern that the minimum wage has encouraged some employers to take on illegal workers and there is also evidence that certain criminal gangs recruit illegal workers through newspaper advertisements in Eastern Europe. Whatever the exact number and nature of the illegal workforce, in 2000, 47,000 illegal entrants were detected.

This, then, is the first major issue that Britain faces with regard to asylum: the issue of legality and justice. The asylum system does not work as smoothly as it should. It is easily exploited by those whose applications fail, by those who use it as a last resort after their illegal presence has been detected and by those who make money enabling such exploitation.

Quite apart from the fundamental moral issues at stake here, the implications of this failure are far reaching. Illegal employment often amounts to little more than slave labour. Those who exist in the shadows of failed asylum applications are themselves often at the mercy of the unscrupulous. Public services, not least the health service, find themselves under increased pressure.

More subtly, but no less worrying, such exploitation and inefficiency provoke public hostility. Conducting research into the future of retirement for The Tomorrow Project in the summer of 2003, I was treated to frequent diatribes on corrupt asylum seekers, many of whom were blamed for the perceived state pension crisis.

> We are quite prepared to give it [i.e. benefit support] to some bugger that comes here from wherever, who has contributed nothing in any way, shape or form. (Male, 50s, Nottingham)

Reactions like this were not atypical and, more pointedly, not voiced by some BNP fringe faction but by respectable 'middle Englanders'. Not only do such visceral opinions tar the innocent with the stain of the guilty but, more alarmingly, they bode ill for any period of economic downturn when, as history has shown, immigrants, especially those whose legality is in question, often bear the brunt of indigenous despondency. Without a just, legal and efficient system, everyone, particularly the most vulnerable, ends up suffering.

Mercy and humanity: the treatment of asylum applicants

The one issue which excites people as much as the idea of an inefficient system being exploited by the un-scrupulous is the thought of vulnerable individuals, whose lives have already been torn apart by injustice, being ignored, maltreated, demonised and rejected by a supposedly hospitable nation. For some asylum applicants, their ordeal is far from over when they arrive in the UK. At best they are reduced to a controversial statistic; at worst they are portrayed as deceptive, faceless scroungers. An efficient, just and legal system is not enough if the society on behalf of which it acts is hostile and inhospitable.

This tension comes to a point in the treatment of asylum applicants. The fact that there are many disingenuous asylum claims every year has become tacit justification, in some quarters at least, for viewing and treating asylum applicants with less than their full human dignity. Whilst most people would agree that this is wrong, exactly how applicants should be treated is an altogether different matter. As ever, reality is not as tidy as theory.

Questions can be asked of the process at virtually every stage. How soon after their arrival in the UK should asylum applicants be expected to submit their claim? At what point, if at all, does a delayed claim become invalid? Should those who claim asylum after having been found working illegally be treated in the same way as those who claim at a seaport at the moment of their arrival?

Following the immediate arrival and/or application for asylum, there are questions about the right means and period of 'accommodation', 'induction' or 'detention' (depending on your preferred term). Should asylum applicants be detained in accommodation centres at all? If so, what is an acceptable time frame for this stage in the process? If not, how and where should asylum applicants be dispersed? What safeguards and guarantees should there be that they will keep in contact with the relevant authorities? How should they best receive healthcare?[24] What is the appropriate level and means of payment that asylum applicants should receive in the meantime and how far should they be encouraged or compelled to integrate into society?

There is particular controversy about this stage. While there was consensus over the abolition of the asylum voucher scheme, which was unpopular and widely regarded as mendacious,[25] there is far less agreement over the need for 'induction' or 'accommodation' centres. On the one hand, organisations like the Refugee Council and the Churches' Commission for Racial Justice (CCRJ) have 'consistently opposed the detention of asylum seekers in secure centres', and the confinement of asylum applicants in prisons was widely condemned as unjustifiable and illegal. On the other hand, the experiences of the BBC Panorama journalist described above suggest that the absence of any official accommodation can leave applicants dangerously vulnerable to isolation, homelessness, hunger, and the 'help' of criminal organisations, while virtually giving official sanction to those who intend to dodge the system.

The introduction of Application Registration Cards is also controversial. These are plastic 'smartcards' which hold applicants' biometric data, such as their personal details, photograph, fingerprint and permission (or lack of it) to work in the UK. Whilst their intention is to streamline the application procedure and deter abuse of the system, CCRJ has described them as 'a cause for concern'.

> While the Home Secretary has given assurances to Parliament that the smart card would ensure access to some cash element, this policy appears to be divisive, clearly separating out one group in society. We are opposed to moves that would see the ARC being used to determine asylum seekers' entitlement to universal services such as health and education.[26]

The application process itself is open to question. At what stage and to what extent should applicants have access to legal advice?[27] What minimum standard should there be for the interpreters used throughout the process?[28] What assistance should be given with the extensive Statement of Evidence form which applicants are required to complete?[29] What right of appeal should applicants have? How valid is the Home Office's 'white list' of safe countries to which applicants are returned without right of appeal?[30] To what extent is there and should there be a 'culture of disbelief' in the application and appeals process?

This is just a handful of the detailed issues facing the government and the nation if we want to implement a procedure that is compassionate as well as efficient.[31] Questions can also be asked of the appeals process, the return and resettlement policy and the overall nature of support throughout the whole procedure.[32] Equally importantly, there are many issues concerning the integration of successful asylum applicants with mainstream society, their treatment by the UK-born population and their portrayal in some sections of the media.

It is simply not enough for a system to be efficient and well-structured, particularly if that system is marked by a sense of reluctant acquiescence rather than positive welcome, and works on behalf a nation which is inherently hostile to all applicants.

Conclusion: underlying issues

Many of the issues discussed above will sound specific and policy focused. Border controls, accommodation centres and resettlement policy are complex, specialised and, above all, contemporary issues. To turn to biblical teaching to address any of these is surely perverse, given that each is a distinctly modern issue.

What is too infrequently recognised, however, is that all policies, no matter how detailed, ultimately rest on value judgements that are not only 'timeless' but also axiomatic. They cannot be *proved* right or wrong by any process of logic or reason but nevertheless form the foundations on which (hopefully) logical and rational policies are then built.

Our response to many of the issues discussed above concerning the justice, legality, mercy, and humanity of asylum today will be shaped by the sociological data on, for example, the impact of the asylum voucher scheme or the results of dispersal policy. But it will be equally influenced by more intangible factors.

What is our national and individual responsibility to those in need? Are we as a nation bound to treat those born abroad in the same way as those born in the UK and, if not, how should treatment differ? How does our responsibility to asylum applicants relate to our responsibility to the existing underprivileged in our society? How do we define and foster human dignity in our treatment of both sets of people?

How far should our much-vaunted tolerance stretch? How far should the illegal actions of the desperate be tolerated? Should our attitude to people-trafficking be shaped by a desire to punish, deter or rehabilitate the criminal?

What is the appropriate tone and language to use of asylum applicants? It may be technically correct to run the headline, as one broadsheet did in June 2003, 'Aids-infected asylum seekers "overwhelm UK hospitals"', but given the febrile atmosphere which surrounds the issue, is it *right* to do so?[33]

What is our role vis-à-vis the rest of the world? Do we have any right to interfere in domestic situations that indirectly affect the UK as many do? If so, how, by what means and with whose permission?

Perhaps most fundamentally, what is our attitude to asylum applicants? Do we see them as a threat, a blessing or a problem? And by the same reckoning, what is our attitude to our own society? Do we see it as, or want it to be, autonomous, organic, pure, unchanging, dynamic, flexible, or fragmented?

These questions underpin the way we think about asylum in the UK and touch on enormous, abstract topics, such as responsibility, dignity, tolerance, freedom and sovereignty. Each has a long history of thought and debate propping up the various responses that dominate the current political landscape, concepts such as human rights, the international order, national sovereignty and freedom of speech.

These modern responses are by no means wrong – indeed the defining characteristic of such issues is that no answer can be *proved* wrong – but they are not necessarily recognisably Christian. Nevertheless, being abstract and value based they are open to a Christian critique, with the challenge to Christians being not only to develop a biblical mind by means of which they might evaluate modern value statements but also to explore how the appropriate biblical foundations might themselves be translated into policy.

The number of asylum applicants

One question in particular may be conspicuous for its absence in the above discussion. Given the quarterly publication of Home Office figures, the comparisons this encourages, and the vivid analogies it permits ('the population of Cambridge every year'), it is hardly surprising that one of the most frequently asked questions is, 'How many asylum applicants should the UK accept?'

This is, however, the wrong question to ask. In spite of Tony Blair's famous and nearly successful promise in October 2002 to halve the number of asylum applications in a year, setting targets for an issue where so many of the most important drivers are out of domestic political control is difficult. As already observed, domestic policy does make some difference, as the fall in UK applications between 2002 and 2003 has shown, but the fact remains that 'short of massive pre-emptive action in other countries, [a government has] no control over the potential numbers coming forward to claim their right under the 1951 Geneva Convention.'[34] Measures such as 'new UK border controls in France ... tackling the continuing problems of asylum applicants lodging groundless appeals to frustrate the process and ... moving to a single tier of appeal'[35] clearly make a difference, but at the end of the day the issue is too big for any one government to have the tools to deal with it comprehensively.

The question is also wrong, however, because it separates the number of asylum applications from the broader and more complex question of the number of immigrants, to which we now turn.

3. Issues of Immigration

Setting the scene

All asylum applicants are immigrants but not all immigrants are asylum applicants.

The immigrant category is considerably more heterogeneous than is often recognised, incorporating foreign nationals who arrive for reasons of asylum, family reunion and work schemes, UK nationals returning home after a period spent abroad, and individuals who come to the UK on a temporary basis, to study, visit relatives or in transit and then extend their stay.[1]

Generally speaking, the intention to remain resident within the UK for a period of at least 12 months is the basic criterion for inclusion, although given changes of circumstances this is not always predictable. Either way, the category still incorporates American CEOs, Armenian asylum applicants, Egyptian heart surgeons, Nigerian hospital porters, Swedish au pairs resident for a few years, West Indian OAPs resident for over five decades, Bangladeshi relatives who cannot speak English, and Canadian ones who can speak nothing but. It is, by anyone's reckoning, a diverse group of people.

Recognising this diversity is important, not simply as a means of preparing us for the complexity of the issue, but also as a way helping us avoid the over-simplifications that confuse the debate. Immigrants are not the same as asylum applicants. Immigration does not correspond to ethnicity. Immigrants are not necessarily Muslims or, indeed, any other religious group. They are not all poor. They do not all speak bad English. They do not all have valuable labour skills. Indeed, any universal statement concerning immigrants is almost guaranteed to be as wrong as a corresponding statement about British nationals. Each group is too broad and diverse to permit easy generalisations.

The danger of oversimplification starts with the popular story of post-war immigration that provides the backdrop for the current debate. It is this story to which we now turn, before proceeding to examine the contours of the contemporary debate on this complex and many-sided issue.

Migration past and future: the context

The story of post-war migration is well known.[2] In the immediate post-war period, substantial immigration from the Commonwealth was encouraged so as to redress labour shortages and help with national reconstruction. Immigration levels grew throughout the 1950s with nearly half a million Commonwealth citizens arriving in Britain between 1955 and 1962.

Domestic racial antagonism also increased, however, culminating in riots against coloured immigrants in September 1958. This ugly development helped precipitate increasingly restrictive immigration legislation, beginning with the Commonwealth Immigrants Act in 1962 which removed the right of Commonwealth citizens born outside the UK or without UK passports to enter the UK freely. Three years later there was a further tightening of the act, reducing the number of entry vouchers available to Commonwealth citizens born outside the UK, and in 1968 another act strengthened controls still further, removing the automatic right of entry for British passport holders. At around this time immigration from India and subsequently Bangladesh began to outpace that from the Caribbean.

The early 1970s saw a further immigration act that replaced employment vouchers with work permits, and the arrival, after some vacillation by the Heath government, of around 40,000 British passport-carrying Ugandan Asians who had been expelled by Idi Amin. It also saw a consensus, in some quarters at least, that immigration policy had been (implicitly) settled on the basis that there was to be no more non-white immigration except for some family reunion, no major changes to or public discussion of the immigration system, no repatriation of immigrants or their descendants, and the promotion of equal opportunity and anti-racism so as to facilitate the integration of non-white immigrants and their children.[3]

The reality was, of course, rather different, with immigration growing continuously throughout the 1980s and 1990s, continued public interest (bordering on obsession) with immigration policy, and several high-profile racist crimes that raised many questions about the extent and success of the ethnic and cultural integration. The story of post-war immigration has not been especially happy and is by no means complete.

Whilst largely accurate, this popular story is far from the whole truth. Rather misleadingly, it assumes a somewhat narrow view of migration, in particular with regard to permanence, provenance and balance.

As already been observed, the concept of the migrant is not a simple one. As the Home Office study *International Migration and the United Kingdom* says, 'there is no consensus on what migration is ... there is no legal definition of "immigrant" in the UK ... the concept of [a] labour migrant is equally unclear ... [and] types of migration are not immutable.'[4] The criteria which are used – 'foreignness', citizenship, birthplace, country of last/next residence and ethnicity – say nothing of the permanence of an immigrant's situation, other than the fact that a migrant must declare his or her intention to remain in the UK for more than one year. This can lead to confusion between immigration and permanent settlement. This history of post-war migration is not simply that of individuals and families settling in Britain *permanently* but includes students, au pairs, work permit holders, and their dependants, who remain for a specified length of time, the total number of whom far outweighs the number of acceptances for settlement (383,000 vs. 97,120 in 1999, for example).[5]

The history of post-war migration is also far broader than the story of individuals and families from the New Commonwealth (the loose group of nations which emerged out of decolonisation) moving to Britain. Whilst this pattern may have been dominant in the immediate post-war period, with Britain's membership of the EEC in the 1970s and the growing emphasis on a global skills market from the 1980s, this completely changed. Between 1981 and 1999, only 17 per cent of immigrants to Britain came from the New Commonwealth, roughly the same as came from the EU, and rather fewer than came from other nations (i.e. those not in the EU, or Old or New Commonwealths).[6]

Acknowledging this is far from a purely academic exercise. One of the biggest dangers of the popular post-war immigration story is that it confuses the issues of ethnicity and immigration and thus leads to British-born non-white people being wrongly classed as immigrants, and foreign-born white people as being wrongly classed as Britons. Recognising the wider provenance of immigrants helps disentangle this confusion, explodes the careless use of ethnicity statistics to explain immigration policy, and reminds us that it is wrong to label those who take a pro- or anti-immigration stance as necessarily anti-British or racist.

The popular story also overlooks the fact that, at least until the mid-1980s, high levels of emigration more than balanced those of immigration. Between 1951 and 1981, the total net international migration for the UK was around *minus 35,000* people, i.e. 35,000 more people left the UK to live abroad than arrived to live there during this period of supposed high-level immigration. Only since the mid-1980s has immigration exceeded emigration in any consistent and significant way. All too often, Britain's post-war history is portrayed as an exercise in 'importing' new people, and little attention is paid to the significant 'export' of British citizens.

Post-war British migration is, therefore, a complicated phenomenon and cannot be reduced to the story of coloured immigrants from ex-dominion nations settling in Britain. It is one in which national boundaries have become increasingly permeable to people, just as they have to capital. It is one shaped by people's short-term desire for new experiences just as much as by their long-term plans for relocation. And it is one influenced by new international agreements, such as the development of the European Union, just as much as by 'old' historic relationships.

It is also a story that cannot be told in isolation from the rest of Europe or the developed world. The last two decades have seen the emergence of a global migration market, mainly for the highly skilled.[7] Starting with the Australian and Canadian governments in the 1980s, the US government in the early 90s, and then latterly Western European governments, competition for 'highly skilled' workers has become intense. Perceived specific skills shortages, particularly in IT and certain public services, especially health and education, have driven a particular kind of international migration. The spread of corporate giantism, the globalisation of Western media and the growth of cheap, accessible telecommunication technology have also advanced the global skills market.

Understanding exactly how these factors will shape future movement of people is by no means easy. Predicting migration trends is notoriously difficult, as previous forecasts testify. The 1991 government predictions, for example, reckoned that the then current net inflow of 50,000 people per annum would increase to 65,000 by 1993–94 and then decline to zero by 2015.[8]

That said, many of the drivers behind the significant increase of the last decade seem certain to intensify. Globalisation, European economic integration, increased labour mobility, improved communication, and cheaper and easier travel will make the free movement of people easier and more attractive. The persecution and poverty driving the asylum element of immigration is less certain to increase, but even the (highly unlikely) satisfactory settlement of the world's 12 million convention refugees over the next decade is unlikely to offset the trend towards international migration. Whilst this general trend need not be directly correlated to immigration in Britain, the links are sufficiently strong for one Home Office report to draw the conclusion:

While there may be some decline from the unusually high net migration levels of the last few years, the long-term secular trend is likely to be increasing for at least the medium term ... we know that higher migration flows are likely to be persistent: both because migrants acquire legal rights around family reunion, and because of chain migration effects.[9]

Specific forecasts may vary (from 135,000 to 250,000 per year, for example[10]) and, as seen from the 1991 projection, are far from infallible, but no one believes as they did in the 1970s that immigration is a closed issue. The overwhelming historic precedent of British emigration, combined with the rise of globalisation making national borders increasingly permeable to money, skills, needs and people, mean that immigration is almost certain to become one of the dominant national and international issues of the twenty-first century.

Contours of the debate*

The size, diversity and history of the UK's immigrant population mitigate against a simple, clearly-drawn list of questions which might define the entire debate. Those most frequently asked – What is the right level of immigration? Is immigration policy 'working'? What should be demanded of immigrants and of host communities? – are not only delicately intertwined but touch on a wide range of issues, the most important of which are demographics, economics, society, environment, culture and international relations.

* The following sections draw on Anthony Browne's excellent study *Do we need mass immigration?* (London: Civitas, 2002).

It is to these six areas that we turn in order to understand the contours, or more accurately in this instance, the layers of the contemporary debate, before once again examining the principles and values which underpin it.

Demographics: the 'right' number

One of the commonest questions asked in the immigration debate – What is the right level of immigration? – is also one of the most misleading. There is no *right* level of immigration in any absolute or verifiable sense. No single annual figure could possibly be the sole, demonstrably correct one, even if all the relevant data were known. As with so many aspects of the asylum and immigration debate, personal value systems and worldviews play far too important a role to permit any single, simple solution.

Having said that, nobody doubts that there are plenty of *wrong* levels. Most people, but particularly those concerned with cultural diversity, believe that zero immigration would have a stultifying effect on national culture. Alternatively, many people, particularly those concerned with environmental issues, feel that high levels of immigration would be disastrous for the nation's natural environment. The level of immigration is, therefore, one of those strange questions to which there is no right answer but plenty of wrong ones.

Recognising this obliges us to stop talking about the *right* level of immigration and start talking about the *optimum* one. The change of word may seem trivial but its implications are profound. No longer are we searching for the elusive, unprovable and ultimately highly subjective 'correct' answer. Instead, having recognised this for the chimera it is, we are looking for the best possible one. We are compelled into a debate that is inherently open, demands that we show our 'value' workings, invites us to learn from opposing viewpoints and, above all, helps us to circumvent the hubris of much political posturing in this area. It also insists we maintain the humility of recognising that any answer we arrive at will not be the only one that a sane person could possibly hold.

Of all levels of the immigration debate, this demographic one should, in theory, be the most straightforward. Over the last 20 years, the population of the UK has increased by around 2.5 million, nearly half of which (1.17 million) has come from net inward migration, almost all of which was in the 1990s.[11] The remaining population growth has been natural, i.e. more births than deaths, the rate of which currently stands at around 60,000 per year.[12]

This natural increase seems strange at first, given that the total fertility rate (TFR) currently stands at 1.64 and has been below the replacement level (i.e. the level at which a nation's population would remain naturally static) for roughly 30 years.[13] In reality, net inward migration has helped reinvigorate natural population growth, not least because it is believed that immigrants have, on average, a higher TFR than the UK-born population.[14]

This gradual increase, powered jointly by immigration and birth, is forecast by the Government Actuary's Department (GAD) to continue over the next twenty years.

> The UK population is projected to increase gradually from an estimated 59.2 million in 1998 to reach 63.6 million by 2021, equivalent to an annual growth rate of 0.3 per cent. Longer-term projections suggest the population will peak around 2036 at almost 65 million and then start to fall. Just over half the projected 4.4 million increase in the population

between 1998 and 2021 is directly attributable to migration.
The remainder is due to natural increase (more births than
deaths).[15]

The inherent unpredictability of migration within this
forecast introduces some uncertainty into the debate and
has caused national population projections to be revised
upwards on several occasions over recent years when
immigration levels were far higher than originally
anticipated. However, with GAD forecasts based on the
assumption of annual net migration of +135,000,[16] it is
hoped that current projections are accurate and will not
need to be revised upwards.[17] In any case, annual net
immigration combined with natural population growth
suggests that the popularly anticipated 'demographic
timebomb' is something of a myth. The *only* situation in
which the Office for National Statistics envisions any
such 'timebomb' is their extreme 'LP' scenario of 'low
fertility, low migration and low life expectancy'.[18]

The real demographic debate is less about population
levels in themselves, however, and more about their
internal dynamic and the impact that this is likely to have
on society. The issue is not so much that the national
population is forecast to increase by four or so million
over the next two decades but that the balance within the
population is changing. Life expectancy at birth is
currently 76 for men and 80 for women and is expected to
increase to 81 and 85 respectively by 2031.[19] At the same
time, the national average age is projected to increase
from 38.2 (in 2002) to 43.3 (in 2031),[20] the number of
children aged under 16 to fall by 7.4 per cent by 2014 (and
then to rise slowly until the late 2020s),[21] and the number
of people over pensionable age to reach 15 million by
2031.[22]

These internal changes have been widely reported and
have caused something approaching national consterna-

tion, with popular opinion talking of a 'dependency ratio crisis', and envisioning some form of social meltdown as the population ages and those working are no longer able to support those retired. The reality is, as ever, slightly more complex. According to GAD:

> The dependency ratio, the ratio of children aged under 16 and adults of pensionable age (allowing for the change in the state retirement age of women) to people of working age, is expected to fall gradually from 628 dependents per 1,000 working age people in 1998 (after a peak of 721 in 1974) to about 580 in 2020. It will then increase rapidly, with longer-term projections suggesting a levelling off around 700 from the mid-2030s.[23]

This, as the quotation hints, is mainly due to the impending increase in women's pension age, followed by a sharp rise in the number of people of pensionable age, as the 1960s baby boomers retire.

As the quotation also indicates, however, demographics may be the initial and most obvious level in the immigration debate, but it is, in reality, little more than the introduction to other levels. The issue is not so much about population size or even population distribution, but rather the relationship between those factors and others, such as the economy.

Economics: making immigration work

It is a widely held belief that immigration is good for a nation's economy. A 2001 Home Office analysis of the economic and social effects of migration concluded its section on 'the economic theory of migration' tentatively but positively.

> It is extremely difficult to estimate empirically the effect of migration on economic growth across countries, for two

reasons. First, migration does not 'cause' growth: the relationship is likely to run in both directions. Second, growth is affected by numerous other factors, and identifying the effect of migration is far from trivial ... [Nevertheless, our] results suggest that, as theory would predict, migration has had positive effects both on growth and on growth per capita. A one per cent increase in the population through migration is associated with an increase in GDP of between 1.25 and 1.5 per cent. *It should be emphasised that this type of analysis must be regarded as suggestive at most.*'[24] [Emphasis original]

On the back of this conclusion, a more specific analysis published the following year came up with an equally tentative estimate for the contribution that immigrants had made to the UK economy.

It is estimated that in 1999/2000 migrants in the UK contributed £31.2 billion in taxes and consumed £28.8 billion in benefits and state services, a net fiscal contribution of approximately £2.5 billion after rounding. This is equivalent to around 1p on the basic rate of income tax.[25]

This is an important and widely quoted figure, although one that fails to take into account additional infra-structure costs and that the report is careful to contextualise.

The UK-born population was also estimated to have paid more in taxes than it received in terms of public services and welfare in 1999/2000 (by just under 5 per cent), reflecting a surplus in the public sector accounts. Migrants made a net contribution estimated at just under 10 per cent.[26]

This fine balance (from which the researchers are understandably nervous about drawing definite con-clusions) reflects the known facts of the immigrant population. A higher proportion of immigrants are of working age than the UK-born population. Accordingly, a lower proportion is retired and draws the state pension.[27] Immigrants earn, on average, a higher wage, being slightly under-represented in each of the lowest three income categories (£0–100, £101–200 and £201–300 per week gross) and over-represented in all the others, particularly those at the top end of the scale (£801–900, £901–1000 and £1,001+ per week gross).[28]

Conversely, a lower proportion of working age immigrants is employed and a higher proportion claims income support and unemployment benefit. Similarly, a higher proportion of immigrants claims child benefit and housing/council tax/rent rebates.[29] The resulting if tentative bottom-line figures reflect this delicate balance.

Whilst this is true of the *overall* immigrant population, it is important to recognise that the nationwide picture obscures important differences. The immigrant population of the UK is an economically polarised one. As the fiscal analysis paper states:

> Data comparing the wages of UK-born residents and migrants in employment suggests that, overall, migrants perform somewhat better than the UK-born – in aggregate migrants receive 12 per cent more in wage income – but it is clear that this average result disguises highly varied performance within the migrant population.[30]

This is hardly surprising, given the size and heterogeneity of the immigrant population. Immigrants earn more but are more likely to be economically inactive. A lower proportion is employed but a higher proportion is self-employed.[31] Ethnic minority immigrant groups have average wages over 10 per cent *lower* than the UK-born population, compared with the overall immigrant difference, which is 12 per cent higher.[32]

In spite of these internal variations, the overall positive effect of immigration on the economy appears to recommend increased immigration. The dependency ratio may be forecast to improve in the immediate future but the long-term prospects seem to demand a strong economy underpinned by a growing workforce. The answer, therefore, to the question asked by a United Nations Report of the same title, 'Is replacement migration a solution to declining and ageing populations?'[33] appears to be yes.

The logic of this reasoning is impeccable, yet the conclusion drawn is sustainable only in the short term. Immigrants, in spite of their net fiscal contribution, also age. The point is widely recognised, for example in the Spring 2001 edition of Population Trends:

> Despite much recent attention being focused on migration, it is clear that this is not a long-term solution to the 'problems' of population ageing … [34]

and a Home Office study of the same year:

> the impact of immigration in mitigating population ageing is widely acknowledged to be small because migrants also age. For a substantial effect, net inflows of migrants would not only need to occur on an annual basis but would have to rise continuously.[35]

and the UN study mentioned above:

> The levels of migration needed to offset population ageing (i.e. maintain potential support ratios) are extremely large, and in all cases entail vastly more immigration than occurred in the past. Maintaining potential support ratios at current levels through replacement migration alone seems out of reach, because of the extraordinarily large numbers of

migrants that would be required. In most cases, the potential support ratios could be maintained at current levels by increasing the upper limit of the working-age population to roughly 75 years of age.[36]

As these latter two quotations indicate, the problem is not the theory, which is sound, but the practical consideration that to maintain the ratio which increased immigration achieves in the first place, would demand exponentially greater immigration as each generation of immigrants ages. The figures involved, thus, swiftly become absurd.

The UN calculates that to maintain the UK dependency ratio, the UK would need to have 59,775,000 immigrants by 2050, increasing the population to 136 million. At the end of that period, immigration would need to be running at 2.2 million a year, and still growing exponentially. To carry on this strategy of replacement migration, the UK would then need to import about another 130 million by 2100, doubling the population to about a quarter of a billion.[37]

Because economics is not a zero-sum game, economies can grow *ad infinitum* if there are the people and resources to fuel them. The UK could theoretically operate a successful economy of 4.5 million people, like Norway, or of nearly 300 million, like the US, the limiting criteria coming not in human but in social and environment factors. The result is that, just as the demographic level of the debate directed us towards the economic one, the economic one requires us to look at social and environmental factors.

There are, in addition to these broad, macro level economic arguments, important micro issues that also need to be considered.

The overall economic success of immigration should not blind us to the significant variations within the immigrant population, which are best seen when the data are analysed along ethnic lines. Immigrants from white ethnic backgrounds tend to perform as well as or better than the existing population in terms of their employment and incomes, whereas those from ethnic minority backgrounds tend do worse than the UK-born population.

Rates of pay also vary between minority ethnic groups. Pakistani and Bangladeshi employees earn less than any other group – around 30 per cent below the national average.[38] A household of Pakistani or Bangladeshi background is four times more likely to be low income than a white household (60 per cent vs. 16 per cent).[39] The income of other ethnic minority groups falls around 10 per cent behind white workers, although some, such as Chinese men and women, and Caribbean women earn more, on average, than white men and women respectively.[40]

It should be emphasised that the use of ethnicity data at this juncture is not a careless breaking of the golden rule of analysis that ethnic minority data and should not be used in place of immigration data. Instead, it is a recognition that the impact of immigration policies does not end with the first generation of immigrants. Economic success is passed on and often intensified through generations and therefore, in the absence of any official data for second and third generation immigrants, ethnicity data are the best proxy available.[41]

The variety within these data strongly suggests that the economic success or failure of immigrants has little to do with the fact they are immigrants and far more to do with other factors, and this has been borne out by other studies, which highlight the importance of the following:

- *Education.* Not surprisingly, this has a generally positive effect on employment and participation for immigrants.
- *Qualifications.* Where a particular qualification obtained is influential. UK qualifications are more highly valued in the labour market than those obtained abroad.
- *English language fluency.* Several studies have shown that the employment rate for ethnic minority immigrants is 20–25 per cent higher when they are fluent in English and that the average wage rate is higher too.[42]
- *Time since migration.* Asylum seeking immigrants are not permitted to work when they first enter the country. Broadly speaking, immigrants' employment levels increase the longer they stay in the UK.
- *Knowledge of the UK labour market and relevant work experience.* Both improve employment level considerably.
- *Discrimination.* There is good evidence to believe that the higher than average proportion of self-employed immigrants reflects a historic and possibly current prejudice against employing people from certain ethnic backgrounds.

These different factors are primarily social, educational and cultural, showing once again how different layers in the immigration debate interact with one another.

The flip side to this question of micro-economic impact is the effect immigration has on UK-born workers. Whereas the macro impact can be seen in the estimated £2.5 billion net surplus which immigrants contribute to the economy, this obscures a very particular debate over whether poorer, native-born employees suffer from immigration, to the benefit of richer employers.

The logic behind this was explained by Professor Richard Layard of the London School of Economics in a letter to *The Financial Times* in May 2002.

'Europe needs immigrants, skilled and unskilled', you say. This may now be the conventional wisdom, but it glosses over the conflicts of interest between different groups of Europeans.

For European employers and skilled workers, unskilled immigration brings real advantages. It provides labour for their restaurants, building sites and car parks and helps to keep these services cheap by keeping down the wages of those who work there.

But for unskilled Europeans, it is a mixed blessing. It depresses their wages and may affect their job opportunities. Already unskilled workers are four times more likely to be unemployed than skilled workers, and it is not surprising that they worry.

Although the total size of the labour force has no effect on the unemployment rate, its structure does; and a rise in the proportion of workers who are unskilled does raise overall unemployment. By the same token we do need more immigration of skilled workers, to rebalance our workforce.

But the main argument for unskilled immigration is the interests of the immigrants, not those of 'Europe'. It is not helpful to say that 'Europe needs unskilled immigration', as if all the Europeans were the same. We need to allow for the different interests at stake.[43]

Much anecdotal evidence and some academic studies support this hypothesis.[44] However, there are also studies which disagree with it. For example, this is from the Home Office study *Migrants in the UK: their characteristics and labour market outcomes and impacts.*

Although simple traditional economic theory suggests that expanding the labour supply will drive down wages,

allowing output to increase and raising GDP overall, in
practice, the picture – and the statistical results – suggest a
much more complex set of interactions ... The data on wages
is less reliable and the conclusions must therefore be treated
with some caution ... [but] immigration is found to have, if
anything, a positive effect on the wages of the existing
population – using the most robust data source which is
available, an increase in immigration of one per cent of the
non-migrant population leads to a nearly two per cent
increase in non-migrant wages.[45]

Whilst it seems reasonably clear then that immigration
'works' for the native economy overall, the jury appears
still to be out regarding localised effects, particularly
those concerning unskilled labour.

The economic level of the immigration debate is,
therefore, made up of various different factors. On the
macro side, immigration almost certainly has a positive
effect on a nation's economy, though this does not make it
a sustainable option in the pursuit of ongoing economic
growth. On the micro side, immigrants have varying
levels of economic success, which hinge on a variety of
social, cultural and educational factors, whilst UK
employers undoubtedly benefit and low-income UK
employees possibly lose out as a result of immigration.

Society: immigration and integration

The social contours of the immigration debate provide us
with a particular problem. The social impact of immigration is much harder to assess than its economic counterpart, partly because it covers a wide variety of factors and
partly because there is no obvious metric with which to
measure success. Terms such as integration and
assimilation are helpful and commonly used but difficult
to define, let alone calculate.

That said, it is painfully easy to recognise where immigration has failed socially, as the riots in Burnley, Bradford and Oldham illustrated. The roots of such conflicts are often primarily economic, something which might be expected given the economic disparity between certain immigrant communities and the wider public. However, the separation of economic and social issues can be rather arbitrary, as is clear from the issue of employment participation.

As we have already noted, the broadly successful immigrant integration within the employment market masks numerous specific causes for concern. If we once again use ethnicity data as a proxy for the absent data on second and third generation immigrants, it is clear that long-term employment integration is not wholly successful. In spring 2002, the unemployment rate for all minority ethnic groups was 10.7 per cent, more than double the 4.7 per cent rate in the white ethnic group. Within this, there were wide variations between minority ethnic groups, with 24.2 per cent of those of Bangladeshi origin, 14.6 per cent of those of Black African origin and 6.2 per cent of those of Indian origin being unemployed.[46] Such differences were often exacerbated between genders, with, for example, roughly three times as many Bangladeshi men as women having a job.

Beyond the *fact* of economic participation, it is worth noting that there is a strong sectoral concentration of immigrants within the UK job market, particularly in health, education, IT, catering and agricultural labour.[47] These concentrations tend to be due not to systemic faults and prejudices within the overall employment market but to sector specific issues. In health and education wages are constrained by policy and there are relatively clear procedures for recognising foreign credentials. In IT and many other professions, wages are unconstrained but the relative flexibility of the work permit system allows companies, many of whom have experienced skill shortages over recent years, to employ immigrants. And in comparatively low paid and insecure sectors like catering and domestic services, at least according to the Home Office, 'unskilled natives are simply unwilling or unable, through lack of the most basic work-related skills (or a lack of mobility), to take the large number of available jobs.'[48]

These various employment data suggest that employment ghettoisation of immigrants, inasmuch as it exists, is due to particular immigrant-friendly structures and policies within certain sectors rather than to systemic prejudice. The data also suggest, however, that a by-product of this sectoral concentration, at least in combination with other social and cultural factors, is a lack of long-term employment integration, with all its implications of economic alienation and social fragmentation.

A second element to the social stratum of the immigration debate is that of education, the litmus test of which is not so much the generally high educational standards of immigrants (who will, of course, have been educated abroad) but more the educational achievement of second and third generation immigrants, for which we must again use ethnicity data as a proxy.

These paint a complex picture which, like the economic evidence, hints at differences within the (second and third generation) immigrant communities just as much as between them and the UK-born population. Evidence suggests that:

- on entry to pre-school, 'children of white UK heritage have the highest mean score in cognitive skills (verbal and non-verbal), with the lowest scores being recorded for Pakistani children even when factors such as parents' educational and occupational classifications are taken into account.';

- pupils from Bangladeshi, black and Pakistani ethnic groups perform less well than other pupils in the key early stages;
- pupils from these same ethnic groups also tend to achieve significantly less by the end of compulsory education, although pupils from Chinese and Indian backgrounds do rather better;
- children of ethnic origin tend to stay longer in education at 16 (85 per cent for ethnic minorities taken altogether vs. 70 per cent for white children);
- participation in higher education is higher for every ethnic group (except black Caribbean) than it is for whites, sometimes considerably so (15 per cent white vs. 46 per cent Chinese, 35 per cent Indian).[49]

As with the economic data, these figures suggest that while there is no direct link between (second and third generation) immigrants and educational success, many immigrant communities underachieve educationally in a way that can easily lead to social alienation.

In a third area of social concern, geographic integration, it is abundantly clear that there is a high concentration of immigrants, and therefore, subsequently, of second and third generation immigrant communities, in a small number of urban areas, supremely London. Over half of all immigrants live in London and the South-East. Sixty per cent of Birmingham's ethnic minority population (again to be used as no more than a proxy) live in seven of the city's 39 wards. Few areas north of the Trent-Severn line have an immigrant population of over 5 per cent.[50]

There are many reasons for this imbalance. London is the UK's biggest labour market. The city has grown in size over the last twenty years when other major UK cities have shrunk. It is closer to major ports-of-entry than any other major city. And, most importantly, it has a wider variety of existing immigrant communities than anywhere else in the country.

The impact of this geographical concentration is ambiguous. On the one hand, such concentrations can increase the pressure on housing markets, transport and other infrastructure, and exacerbate overcrowding, congestion and pressures on scarce green-belt land. On the other hand, they can bring skills, experience and know-how with wider benefits to the UK, and help to regenerate run-down areas. Irrespective of how one evaluates the social consequences of such geographical concentration, it is clear that the results of immigration are more polarised geographically than they are economically, occupationally or educationally.

Finally at the social level, there has been increasing debate in recent years over the issue of political participation and representation of ethnic minority communities in politics.[51] In the Greater London Assembly elections, where ethnic minorities made up around a quarter of the electorate, ethnic minority candidates filled two of the 25 seats. Nationally, only three per cent of counsellors and nine MPs are black or Asian, and of the 87 members of the European Parliament, four are black or Asian. These figures are clearly unrepresentative, although they must not be allowed to encourage the fallacy that only an immigrant can represent an immigrant or an ethnic minority member someone from their own community.

Levels of participation are not as low as those of representation. The Electoral Commission's evaluation of voter engagement among black and minority ethnic communities in the 2001 General Election revealed that some of the highest levels in the country were among Asian communities and some of the lowest among black African and Caribbean communities.[52] Other research showed that people of black African heritage have one of the lowest levels of registration.

That said, ethnic minority turnout rates were affected by generic factors, such as their younger age profile, the higher levels of social and economic deprivation experienced among such groups, and the fact that they predominantly live in urban areas where turnout levels tend to be lower than average. The fact that some of the lowest turnout figures in the country were recorded in largely white populated, inner-city areas strongly suggests that the low turnout among certain ethnic minority groups in 2001 was a socio-economic rather than an ethnic issue.

Another research paper published by the Economic and Social Research Council in September 2003 acknowledged the fact that there were problems with ethnic minority political participation but also found that:

> While there is a wide public concern about the decline in black and ethnic minority political involvement we found a diverse and extensive level of political activity ... this political dynamism is missed in part because the definition of 'the political' is too narrow within mainstream political debate.[53]

The researchers found 'a plurality of patterns of minority political involvement ranging from electoral politics to anti-deportation campaigns to literary circles and musical cultures.'

Whilst such findings are encouraging, indicating that politics, in its broadest and truest sense of civic engagement, is in better health among ethnic minority communities than more mainstream data might at first suggest, they do not eliminate the 'pronounced questioning of the legitimacy of conventional political institutions' among such communities.

At the risk of repetition, it should be re-emphasised that ethnic minority data can be used as no more than a proxy for understanding the long-term social success of immigration. Members of the ethnic minorities are not necessarily immigrants – according to the CRE only 52 per cent of individuals from the ethnic minorities were born outside the UK – just as the majority of immigrants to Britain are white.[54]

Nevertheless, even as proxy data they suggest that the relative lack of ethnic minority figures in 'official' political arenas, and the sense of alienation from mainstream political participation that some groups feel, is too great to allow any complacency about the long-term political integration of immigrants.

Overall, the social contours of the immigration debate are immensely complex. The very fact that there are clear statistical differences between ethnic minority and white groups occupationally, educationally, geographically and politically strongly suggests that, even given the proxy nature of the data, immigration has resulted in notable failings on a social level. This should not lead us to the conclusion that immigrants are necessarily poorer, less well educated, more ghettoised, or politically less interested than the UK population. Many are not. Nor should it leave us believing that the only successful immigrant integration is one where no differences between immigrant and non-immigrant are visible. Such a goal could only be realised through brutal social engineering. However, there should be concern that socially, immigration has not necessarily precipitated integration.

Environment and infrastructure: a nice place to live

Quality of life, it is slowly being realised, is not the same thing as wealth.[55] National affluence is all but worthless if people are afraid to walk out at night, must wait months for routine medical care, have no faith in the education system, and are unable to find any patch of land in which they would remotely wish to spend their time. 'Measures of national welfare suggest that rising GDP in developed countries (sic), including the UK, may now be associated with *declining* well-being.'[56]

Of all the factors that need to be balanced against a strong economy, environmental ones are perhaps the most important. The environment is, in human timescales at least, the ultimate, non-negotiable, zero-sum game, and the one that has gained most notoriety in recent decades.

In its official yearbook, *UK 2003*, the ONS describes the country in these words:

> The United Kingdom is a relatively densely populated country, with 242 people per square kilometre in 2001. The number of households is projected to increase (in England, for example, from 20.2 million in 1996 to 24.0 million in 2021). These changes, together with an increase in the population and the demands of a growing economy, mean there are pressures on land use.[57]

The figure of 242 people per sq. km (which rises to 389 for England and Wales) is less than that of Belgium (337) but exceeds that of Germany (230), Italy (191), France (107) and Spain (79), and the US (29).

Although much new development is planned for brownfield sites and comprises single person households, the fact remains that, as the Campaign to Protect Rural England has said, 'vast areas of countryside and small communities are under threat from Government housing plans.'[58]

Much of the need for new housing, particularly in urban areas, comes not from immigration or natural population growth but the need to house key workers. The substantial rise in house prices over the last decade has effectively priced many key workers (and first-time buyers) out of the housing market in some areas. New housing is often badly needed in these areas to prevent them from becoming residential no-go areas for public sector workers.

The localised dearth of key workers is part of a larger picture in which a number of public sector bodies are critically short of employees and eagerly attracting foreign-born workers to fill their gaps, often much to the irritation of foreign governments. And this broader scarcity is itself part of a larger picture in which the nation's social infrastructure appears in poor health.

Population increase and house building programmes do not (or should not) exist in a vacuum. Despite, or perhaps because of, the increased atomisation of modern life, with the rise of single person households, car ownership, communication technology and enormously sophisticated home entertainment systems, people still crave community and personal interaction.

The social infrastructure which facilitates this – from schools, hospitals and policing to water and sewage systems, effective transport networks, local retailers and community centres – needs to be in place to prevent existing communities from deteriorating and to enable new developments to be anything other than ghost towns.

Evidence detailing the 'success' or 'failure' of social infrastructure is, of course, rather less clear-cut than population or economic data. Yet the public service problems that have dogged the Labour government, not to mention the ideological battles over public service provision which have raged within it, are testimony not only to the importance and lack of consensus which marks this issue, but also to the widespread feeling that whilst the UK may boast one of the world's highest GDP per capita figures, this is not mirrored in its quality of life.

Culture: who do we think we are?

Gauging the cultural impact of immigration makes assessing its economic or social counterpart look easy. The literature on the topic is endless,[59] a fact which is hardly surprising once we recognise that the 'term culture … includes all the characteristic activities and interests of a people.'[60] To examine the success and prospect of cultural integration in the wake of large-scale immigration is little short of asking the question posed by Yasmin Alibhai-Brown's eponymous book, *'Who do we think we are?'*

One of the few things that commentators across political and ideological spectrums agree on today is that one answer to this question is, 'Not who we once thought we were.' The four historic pillars of Britishness – union, empire, monarchy and Protestantism – so central to national identity for so long, have each been severely eroded in the last half-century.

What is particularly important to recognise for our purposes is that this rapid erosion was largely *independent* of post-war immigration. The absence of a common enemy, the ongoing bloodshed in Northern Ireland and the growing economic inequalities across the United Kingdom were enough by themselves to unravel the union. The British Empire was already under obvious stress in the 1940s and was destined to be dismantled in the post-war period along with other European empires.

The monarchy could never have survived intact in a country that now eschewed deference, and in any case did its best to self-destruct in the 1980s and 90s. And the nation was, in fact, only nominally Protestant by the mid-twentieth century, with membership of the established Church standing at around 10 per cent of the population of England and Wales in 1950. Immigration may have acted as a catalyst for the cultural re-evaluation that these changes precipitated but it did not cause it.

The effect of all this has been to complicate the question of cultural integration. With little consensus on what Britishness is, the fundamental issue moves from being the success of cultural integration to its very basis: what degree of cultural integration is appropriate in the first place?

The currently popular, liberal-rooted response to this is to say that any form of compulsion of an individual's cultural identity is unacceptable, but this position is riddled with difficulties. Ultimately, everyone ends up drawing the line at some cultural practice, whether it is with the Hindu practice of sati (the self-immolation of widows),[61] the African practice of clitoridectomy,[62] the Rastafarian use of ganja,[63] the Jewish and Muslim method of animal slaughter for the preparation of Kosher and Halal meat,[64] or the Islamic wearing of head-scarves.[65] Hardly anyone in Britain would defend all of these practices and many people, ironically often those who like to claim the moral high ground of tolerance, would ban all of them.

If cultural omni-tolerance is untenable, however, so is the opposite position of cultural totalitarianism. Just as few people would want to defend sati, few would recommend the ubiquitous state intervention in people's personal lives that characterised Stalin's Russia.

The remaining middle ground is inevitably a marshy one, which threatens to trap anyone who ventures on to it in the fatuousness of 'boutique multiculturalism': energetically celebrating the vibrancy of the international restaurant scene in London yet failing to say anything constructive about creating unity in areas such as those whose riots shocked Britain in 2001.

The growing interest in citizenship provides one potential route through the quagmire. David Blunkett's concern in this area has led to citizenship classes in schools, language and citizenship classes for immigrants, citizenship ceremonies welcoming immigrants, and a proposal for identity cards for all UK nationals. Although not uncontroversial (particularly the last of these), these measures may be a step towards balancing the extremes and providing a framework for integration without being culturally dictatorial at the same time. As Bernard Crick, the guiding mind behind much of Blunkett's thinking on these issues, has said, 'We are not trying to define Britishness. We are trying to define what people need to settle in effectively.'

Such a resolution, if it were ever reached, would do nothing to settle the debates over specific cultural praxes, such as those about headscarf wearing in France and Germany, or Halal and Kosher meat preparation in the UK. But it might provide parameters inside which the ongoing questions of cultural integration could be fruitfully discussed.

International relations: the repercussions of immigration

The final, often overlooked element within the immigration debate is the issue of international repercussions.

Immigration does not happen in a vacuum. Every immigrant is also an emigrant. This can be viewed positively: not only do migrant workers realise personal ambitions and higher salaries but they send considerable sums of money to the relatives they have left behind. This global remittance market is estimated at $60 billion a year and is considerably better targeted than many conventional aid programmes.[66]

There is also a cost to this arrangement, however. Quite apart from the fact that remittance-based economies are highly dependent and thus vulnerable, most governments cannot afford to lose their qualified professionals. 'Brain drains' have serious, long-term detrimental effects on both their economies and their social infrastructure.

Ghana, for example, has one of Africa's best, free education systems. Yet about 30 per cent of highly educated Ghanaians choose to live abroad, turning the education system into an excellent, free training programme for many Western countries. The Accra Mail describes the effect of this as follows:

> The unfortunate and demoralising fact in this saga is that, even though the Republic of Ghana continues to invest stupendous amounts of money she can barely afford in the education of its youth, she most tragically does not have much to show for all its aggrandisement, since she has failed to retain the highly skilled workforce ... It seems that our country is 'eaten' by the Western world.[67]

In 2002, economists at Addis Ababa university published a study that claimed that the loss of 20,000 professionals a year from Africa to the West cost the continent about $4 billion per annum.[68] Another study, carried out by the World Health Organisation, the International Council of Nurses and the Royal College of Nursing and published the following year emphasised the particular seriousness of the problem in nursing.[69] So serious is the problem, that sixteen countries, including a number in sub-Saharan Africa have asked the UK to stop recruiting their nurses altogether and ethical guidelines have been put in place in the UK order to stem this 'brain drain.'

The international repercussions of immigration are usually buried beneath the intense political pressure to improve public services and the dominance of neo-liberal orthodoxy that dictates that labour must move to areas of opportunity. Yet the ethical implications of international recruitment are unavoidable. Although many problems lie with foreign economies and public service systems, there are also questions that need to be asked of British policy, the underlying one being, what relationship should exist between the UK and other nations when dealing with the size and nature of the immigrant workforce?

Underlying issues

The debate over immigration in the UK is a vast, unwieldy, multi-layered beast that defies easy definition in spite of some tabloid attempts to prove otherwise. Given that post-war migration has involved the arrival *and departure* of many millions of people, it is hardly surprising that the subject touches on every level of national life.

This chapter will, by its nature, have raised more questions than it has answered. Because those questions which tower over the immigration debate, such as the optimum level of migration or the right policies for successful integration, are so complex, it is important to assess the demographic, economic, social, environmental, cultural and international implications of immigration if we are to grasp the contours of the debate.

Doing so is unlikely to provide us with an 'answer' or even a cogent viewpoint, partly because the terminology is slippery and the data often non-existent, but also partly because, as with asylum, the entire debate rests on 'worldview' foundations, which by their very nature are not empirically verifiable. It is the existence and importance of these underlying principles which validate the very idea of a Christian perspective, and although most Christians will not require such validation, there will inevitably be opposition to any such perspective from those who claim religion has no role to play in the public sphere or who mistakenly believe that all public policy is simply a matter of rational, measurable and technical decisions. Ultimately, all such decisions rest on 'subjective' values and the more cogent these are, the more convincing they will be.

Several key underlying issues stand out. The most elemental of these is what it means to belong. Is belonging a function of birth, location or personal ideology? Is home where I live or where my heart is?

A second question revolves around the eternal tension between individual liberty and cohesive community. How far should I surrender my personal freedom for the sake of the community? What rights does the community have to direct my personal choices?

Third, what is the right 'metric'? Because debates about optimum immigration levels necessarily hinge on the balance between the number of people and some other factor, there is a real question about what that other factor should be. Is economic growth the dominant criterion? Social infrastructure? Available space?

A fourth underlying issue is the vexed question of relative loyalties. What loyalty does one government have to another, in comparison to that which it has to its own population? When fortifying one's own social infrastructure means weakening another nation's, in which direction do principles direct you?

Finally, and more specifically, who do we think we are in the UK today? What validity do the traditional pillars of identity retain? How far and in which direction should national identity be modified in the light of large-scale population movement? What, in short, are we to make of multiculturalism?

There is no guarantee that biblical teaching can provide a convincing answer to any or all of these questions. Indeed, one of the tasks of biblical research is to ascertain what *cannot* (safely) be said, just as much as identifying what can. Rooting out those views which use the Bible to justify rather than shape existing ideologies is a vitally important task, as the theological tensions in pre-war Germany testify all too painfully.

That said, the fact that time and again the relevant questions focus in on *relationships* – between community and individual, between native and immigrant, between population and environment, and between nation and nation – should give us confidence. The Bible is nothing if it is not interested in relationships.

It is with this in mind that we turn to biblical teaching, to see what guidance it offers on the issues of asylum and immigration today.

4. The Relevance of Biblical History

Why the Bible?

Before engaging seriously with biblical teaching on asylum and immigration, it is important to think about why we do so. For many Christians, this will seem, at best, an incidental question. After all, doesn't the Bible enjoin its use in exactly this way?

'These commandments that I give you today,' declares Moses in Deuteronomy 6, 'are to be upon your hearts.' They are to be read and meditated upon at all times and in all places, not for reasons of legalistic piety but 'so that you may enjoy long life.' 'Impress them on your children,' Moses declares. 'Talk about them when you sit at home and when you walk along the road, when you lie down and when you get up. Tie them as symbols on your hands and bind them on your foreheads. Write them on the doorframes of your houses and on your gates.' The law was for everyone, not just criminals and lawyers. As the writer of the great psalm 119 declares:

> I rejoice in following your statutes
> as one rejoices in great riches.

> I meditate on your precepts
> and consider your ways.
> I delight in your decrees;
> I will not neglect your word.[1]

Christ affirmed the principles and role of the Torah, in spite of his anger at the law being turned into a burden rather than a blessing. 'Do not think that I have come to abolish the Law or the Prophets,' he tells disciples in Matthew chapter 5. 'I have not come to abolish them but to fulfil them,' he continues. 'Until heaven and earth disappear, not the smallest letter, not the least stroke of a pen, will by any means disappear from the Law … whoever practises and teaches these commands will be called great in the kingdom of heaven.'[2]

These sentiments were subsequently affirmed in Paul's second letter to Timothy, written at the end of his life. 'All Scripture is God-breathed,' he explains, 'and is useful for teaching, rebuking, correcting and training in righteousness.'[3]

It shall be clear, then, that careful meditation on biblical teaching for the purposes of personal and social edification or, in the words of Deuteronomy, 'so that it may go well with you and your children' is encouraged throughout Scripture.[4]

However, whilst this 'internal' reasoning will be sufficient for many evangelical Christians, it is unlikely to convince those with a lesser opinion of biblical teaching and, more significantly, it does not represent the totality of reasons for turning to the Bible for guidance. It is important to recognise that there are a number of convincing 'external' reasons why biblical teaching and the life of Israel in particular are 'useful' for shaping our thinking on asylum and immigration today.

Israel's geopolitical context

Israel's long and turbulent history cannot be understood without taking into account that of its many, powerful neighbours.[5]

From the time of the Exodus until the destruction of Jerusalem and the beginning of the exile, Israel inhabited a land that was sandwiched between the two international power centres of the Ancient Near East. To the south-west, Egypt had dominated 'global' politics for over a millennium and to the north and north-east the Hittites, Assyrians and then Babylonians had been successive superpowers.

Israel was also sandwiched by two of the main international highways of the period, to the west the coastal highway which ran from Egypt, up the coast of Palestine, then through Galilee and on to Mesopotamia, and to the east the Transjordanian or King's highway which carried traffic north from Edom again towards Mesopotamia.

The result of this pivotal position was that Israel could not help but be in constant contact with foreigners of every ethnic, political, religious, cultural and economic description. The various nations and empires that dominate the pages of the Old Testament comprised four distinct ethnic groups: the Northwest Semites (which included Israel and many of her immediate neighbours), the Egyptians, the Cushites and the Indo-Europeans, and this ethnic makeup expanded still further in New Testament times to include the dozens of Indo-European, Asian and African groups which populated the Roman Empire.[6] Israel was a small player on a stage as ethnically diverse as any we might encounter today.

Similarly, the Israelites rubbed political and economic shoulders with a vast range of foreigners, from the superpowers which enslaved and, half a millennium later, exiled them, through the nations which they dispossessed and with whom they squabbled on an ongoing basis, to the individual traders, immigrants and hired hands who travelled through and lived amongst them. Isolation was simply not an option.

Indeed, isolation was effectively impossible for two reasons. Firstly, there were no international border controls in the modern sense throughout the whole Ancient Near East, thus allowing free movement of peoples in a way inconceivable in the modern West. And second, Israel inhabited a land that lacked natural frontiers and was constantly vulnerable to attack. Biblical teaching on the relationship between the host nation and the alien was rooted in many years of experience.

Israel's origins

More influential than Israel's geopolitical experience was the nation's origins.

Genesis records how, in response to God's call, Abraham left his home in Mesopotamia with the enormous upheaval that would have entailed, and moved to Canaan where his family settled.[7] At its very conception, therefore, 'Israel' witnessed an uprooting and a journey that, for all Abraham's wealth, would have been a traumatic experience.

Throughout this period, Abraham's family did not remain ethnically or politically isolated. Although both Isaac and Jacob returned to Mesopotamia to marry Aramean women,[8] Judah married a Canaanite woman and had twins by another Canaanite woman,[9] Simeon married a Canaanite woman,[10] and Joseph became Pharaoh's chief minister[11] and then married an Egyptian woman, thus giving himself a father-in-law who was the 'priest of On'.[12] As one commentator remarks, 'for much of their history the ethnic boundary between Israel and her neighbours was fuzzy and fluid.'[13]

Nowhere is this better seen than in the story of the Exodus. The account of the Exodus contains one very significant and often overlooked sentence. At the crucial moment, the narrative records that 'many other people went up with them, as well as large droves of livestock, both flocks and herds.'[14] This phrase, innocuously translated in the NIV as 'other people' and more commonly translated as 'a mixed multitude', is most accurately rendered by the rather literal New Living Translation as 'many people who were not Israelites'. The Hebrew term, *'ereb*, makes it clear that these people were non-Israelites who used the opportunity of Israel's exodus to flee Egypt. J. Daniel Hays comments, 'Egyptian literary records ... are replete with references to foreigners in Egypt during this period. [At this time] ... the Egyptians had nominal control over both Cush and Syria-Palestine ... , carried out numerous military campaigns into these regions and brought back thousands of conquered peoples ... as slaves and labourers. It is highly likely that these people constituted the "mixed crowd" of Exodus 12.38.'[15]

The precise number and nature of these 'other people' is not known, but the implication of their presence at this seminal moment of Israelite history is significant. Walter Brueggmann argues that, 'the phrase suggests that this is no kinship group, no ethnic community, but a great conglomeration of lower class folk.'[16] It is no coincidence that the question of whether foreigners, slaves, temporary residents, hired workers and aliens 'living among you' should be permitted to partake of Passover was settled, at least in narrative terms, immediately after the mention of the 'other people'.[17] 'From the start, right relationships with foreigners and aliens was an important and practical issue [for Israel].'[18]

This question did not disappear in the immediate aftermath of the Exodus and, as we shall see, the treatment and welfare of immigrants plays an important role in the Torah. It is highly likely that the foreign population affiliated to and living alongside Israel remained sizeable right up until the exile. In the preparations for building the Temple, Solomon 'took a census of all the aliens who were in Israel', many of whom were involved in the building project.[19] The census counted 153,600 people and although Israelite censuses are not always obviously consistent (2 Samuel 24 and 1 Chronicles 21 differ in their calculation of the number of fighting men, for example), the unarguable fact remains that the foreign population of Israel is likely to have been substantial for many hundreds of years. Biblical teaching on immigration is credible not simply because Israel rubbed shoulders with a spectrum of different peoples but because the nation itself was born with, and lived with, a substantial immigrant population.

Israel's identity

More important than either Israel's geopolitical situation or its origins is the nation's remarkable 'immigrant' identity.

In parallel with Israel's origins, this identity begins in the time of the patriarchs. God's call to Abraham to 'leave your country, your people and your father's household' marks him with the identity of the stranger, a fact which Abraham explicitly acknowledges when arranging for Sarah's funeral: 'Abraham ... spoke to the Hittites [and] said, "I am an alien and a stranger among you. Sell me some property for a burial site here so I can bury my dead."'[20] The writer of the letter to the Hebrews discusses at length how Abraham's willingness to forsake the land and culture that defined him and travel as an alien amongst strangers made him a example of how to live by faith.[21]

It was, however, the subsequent descent into Egypt, the centuries of labour under foreign oppression there and the final, remarkable deliverance from slavery that gave the Israel its unique, immigrant identity.

Having settled in Canaan for two generations, the Israelites found themselves in Egypt through a peculiar combination of criminal abduction and famine-induced desperation. After a brief period as foreigners in Canaan, the family became foreigners in Egypt.

Their initial position of comfort and security was quickly eroded when 'a new king, who did not know about Joseph, came to power,' and began to complain about his nation being flooded by the foreigners whose loyalty he deemed, at best, to be dubious.

> the Israelites have become much too numerous for us ... we must deal shrewdly with them or they will become even more numerous and, if war breaks out, will join our enemies, fight against us and leave the country.[22]

The ensuing oppression did little more than exacerbate the 'problem', however: 'the more they were oppressed, the more they multiplied and spread; so the Egyptians came to dread the Israelites and worked them ruthlessly.'[23] As Jonathan Sacks has remarked, this was the formative time during which the Israelites learned 'from the inside ... what it feels like to be an outsider, an alien, a stranger.'[24]

This experience helped form Israel and marked the nation with a very particular identity of which they were continually reminded: 'you yourselves know how it feels to be aliens, because you were aliens in Egypt ... Love [the alien] as yourself, for you were aliens in Egypt ... you shall declare before the LORD your God: "My father was a wandering Aramean" ... We are aliens and strangers in your sight, as were all our forefathers.'[25] Even on the verge of Canaan and nationhood, they were told, in the starkest terms, that conquest and settlement would change nothing. 'The land must not be sold permanently,' God instructs them, 'because the land is mine and you are but aliens and my tenants.'[26]

Given this insistent emphasis on their intrinsically 'alien' status, it is not entirely surprising that the Hebrew Bible commands the Israelites to love the stranger 'in no fewer than 36 places.'[27]

The coming of Christ changed the situation, although in a far from straightforward way. On the one hand, the resurrection is understood by the New Testament writers to mark not only the end of Israel's exile, which the nation had been eagerly and sometimes violently anticipating, *and* the end of the Gentile's estrangement from God's promises, *but also*, on a grander scale, the beginning of the end of mankind's separation from God. To this extent, as Paul wrote to the church in Ephesus, Gentile Christians 'are no longer foreigners and aliens, but fellow citizens with God's people and members of God's household.'

On the other hand, 1 Peter makes it clear that, whilst no longer being strangers to God, Christian believers remain strangers in the world, a claim that recurs throughout the epistle.

Peter, an apostle of Jesus Christ, to God's elect, strangers in the world, scattered throughout Pontus, Galatia ... live your lives as strangers here in reverent fear ... as aliens and strangers in the world ... abstain from sinful desires.[28]

This theme was central to the early Church's understanding of itself. In the introduction to his so-called first letter to the Corinthians (perhaps the earliest surviving Christian document outside the New Testament), Clement of Rome begins (literally translated), 'From the Church of God which is transiently sojourning in Rome', and in doing so uses a technical term that denotes temporary rather than permanent residence.[29] In a similar fashion, the anonymous writer of the slightly later *Letter to Diognetus* declares:

Though [Christians] are residents at home in their own countries, their behaviour there is more like that of transients; they take their full part as citizens, but they also submit to anything and everything as if they were aliens.[30]

Their 'spiritual' homecoming did not end, and indeed probably exacerbated, their continuing earthly isolation.

An interesting aside to and confirmation of this idea may be seen in the fact that the time when 1 Peter was almost certainly written was one in which the nascent Church, particularly in Rome, was experiencing savage persecution. Christians were believed to be a malign and untrustworthy foreign body whose very existence jeopardised the foundations of the Roman Empire – a prejudice remarkably similar to that of Pharaoh in Exodus chapter 1. Appropriating the identity of the stranger suffering under an oppressive empire must have seemed all too obvious to the letter's author.

However the concept of 'alienation' may have been modified with the incarnation, self-identification with the outsider remained central to the entire biblical canon. Biblical teaching has particular validity on the topic of asylum and immigration because so many biblical writers knew what alienation, exile and dispossession felt like.

Israel's nationhood

Israel's geopolitical situation, origins and identity gave it an acute understanding of the life and trials of the immigrant. The strength of biblical teaching on asylum and immigration comes from the nation's long history and personal experience that bred not just sympathy but empathy.

But Israel, and latterly the Church, had another side to their story that adds a particularly interesting and valuable dimension to the Bible's teaching: the passionate concern to protect and maintain their identity.

As one might expect from their history, Israel welcomed and readily assimilated foreigners. This integration did not demand that foreigners entirely relinquish their original ethnic identity – Ruth, for example, remained 'Ruth the Moabitess' throughout the book which bears her name – but nor did it permit Israel's own ethnic, religious or cultural identity to be diluted or adulterated.

Both these points are important, given the current debate about multiculturalism and the integration of immigrants. Israel not only knew the experience of the immigrant but also the demands of nationhood, and these can be detected throughout the Old Testament. Supremely, it was its position before God and the basic value orientation this precipitated which served to delineate the nation. Faith and ethics were the defining criteria of 'ethnicity', and it was because 'the criterion for community membership was religious ... that foreign sojourners could be so easily assimilated.'[31] This manifested itself in various cultural signs, signals and behaviours, such as worship practice, culinary legislation and intermarriage, through which Israel's distinctive and, given their geopolitical environment, somewhat vulnerable identity was preserved.

The success was varied. On the one hand, biblical law envisages (and probably reflects) the situation where integration has been so successful that the foreigner can be in an economically stronger position than the native Israelite.[32] On the other hand, the repeated warnings against syncretism, immorality and economic injustice throughout the period of the monarchy, show how native Israelites abused and ignored their nation's distinctive identity.

The early Church inherited many of these themes and problems. 'National' signs and symbols were supplanted by the religious and ethical considerations which shaped the earliest Christian communities, which themselves developed distinctive symbols and praxes. That these resulted in as much tension, particularly at the boundary with local culture, as Israel had experienced, is evident from many of Paul's letters. The Church, like Israel, faced the challenge of maintaining borders which were permeable to people but not to values, and it did not always get the balance right. Both Israel and the early Church understood the tensions inherent in community and nationhood just as they did the pains of alienation and immigration.

God's purposes

There is one further reason why we should turn to biblical teaching in order to help us through the minefield of asylum and immigration, and it has nothing to do with either asylum or immigration. Indeed, it is, as it were, a polar opposite to the specificities of the nation and the immigrant.

Over-familiarity with the creation story can blind us to the breathtaking audacity of its message. The axiom to which we unthinkingly cling – that all human beings are of equal worth – is anything but self-evident, despite the assertions of the American Declaration of Independence. Instead it derives from the compelling revelation of Genesis chapter 1, which sets up a human-wide focus that runs through the entire biblical narrative.

Abraham's call in Genesis chapter 12 repeats this – 'all peoples on earth will be blessed through you' – although after the arrogance of Babel it is made clear that this 'universalism' will be on God's terms and not man-kind's.[33] The promise is repeated throughout Genesis[34] and stands at the entrance of the law in Deuteronomy, as Moses says to the Israelites:

> See, I have taught you decrees and laws as the Lord my God commanded me ... observe them carefully, for this will show your wisdom and understanding to the nations, who will hear about all these decrees and say, 'Surely this great nation is a wise and understanding people.'[35]

It hovers in the background of much of the Old Testament but emerges into the brilliant light in Isaiah.

> In the last days the mountain of the Lord's temple will be established as chief among the mountains; it will be raised

above the hills, and all nations will stream to it ... In that day the Root of Jesse will stand as a banner for the peoples; the nations will rally to him ... The Lord will lay bare his holy arm in the sight of all the nations, and all the ends of the earth will see the salvation of our God ... my house will be called a house of prayer for all nations.[36]

This worldwide perspective is, of course, central to the New Testament and reaches its climax in the vision of Revelation, in which the congregation of every tribe, language, people and nation is gathered before the throne of God.[37]

This persistent undercurrent of universal application is important to the immigration debate in two respects. Firstly, it reassures us that no matter how specific the details of the Law and the Prophets, the ultimate concern is for the well-being of everyone on earth. God's plans ignore nobody. Second, as has been pointed out by many commentators, the eschatological visions of Isaiah and John the Evangelist do not abolish distinct community characteristics but instead unite them before God. One has to be slightly careful in this conclusion, as 'all nations' can easily be used as an idiom for 'everyone', but the repeated combination of tribe, language, people and nation in Revelation (the four-fold formula occurs seven times, each time in a different sequence) strongly suggests that these distinct characteristics, which have, after all, done so much to shape individuals, are not disposable irrelevances.

It is, therefore, in this vision that we see reconciled the tension which afflicts so many of the debates on immigration: how do you maintain 'the dignity of difference' within a unified community without succumbing to disintegration on the one hand or totalitarianism on the other?

Using the Bible

Many Christians will recognise the need to turn to biblical teaching for such an important issue without the reasons given above. Others, however, will not and non-Christians will almost certainly need a convincing explanation for such an approach.

Outlining these explanations is valuable not simply for this reason, however. Understanding Israel's unique origins, identity, concept of nationhood, and geopolitical circumstances, many of which were inherited by the early Church, introduce and outline the basic themes, which we now explore in greater detail.

5. Biblical Teaching on 'Asylum' and 'Immigration'*

From immigrants to *gerim*

The first and most important point to make when looking at biblical teaching for guidance on asylum and immigration is that those terms, not entirely clear in modern Britain, are all but meaningless in early Israel. We need to reconsider our categories carefully.

Our modern concept of 'asylum' is dependent on such notions as defined states, secure borders and human rights, none of which can be found in the biblical material. The concept of the 'immigrant' is far less time-bound but, in much the same way as the modern term covers a wide spectrum of situations and usually needs clarification, so the Hebrew Bible has several terms that recognise different kinds of 'alien'.

At one end of the spectrum lie those individuals who are not aliens at all but *'ezrach'* or native Israelites. The word occurs only seventeen times throughout the Old Testament and not at all in Exodus or Deuteronomy,

---

* This chapter draws in particular on *The Status and Welfare of Immigrants* by Jonathan Burnside (Cambridge: Jubilee Centre, 2001)

although its use in Leviticus seems to suggest that it means specifically 'native *of the land*', reflecting the priestly belief in the sanctity of the land.[1]

At the other end were the '*nokrim*' and '*zarim*'.[2] These were 'foreigners' or 'aliens' (which is how the words are usually translated), living in their own country outside the land of Israel. They had no link to the land, people or God of Israel, although they could be connected to the nation economically, as visiting merchants or mercenaries.

Nokrim and *zarim* were regarded with a mixture of suspicion, fear and loathing, and were often seen as enemies, oppressors or plunderers, with whom it was wrong to mix too closely or pursue military alliances.[3] They could be viewed positively, however, and the hope was expressed that they would learn the ways of Israel's God through the example of Israel.

> 'As for the foreigner [nokri] who does not belong to your people Israel but has come from a distant land because of your name – for men will hear of your great name and your mighty hand and your outstretched arm – when he comes and prays toward this temple, then hear from heaven, your dwelling place, and do whatever the foreigner [nokri] asks of you, so that all the peoples of the earth may know your name and fear you, as do your own people Israel, and may know that this house I have built bears your Name.'[4]

In between these two poles, which might be reasonably translated as natives and foreign nationals, there lay the '*ger*' ('*gerim*' in plural) and the '*toshav*'.[5]

Ger is usually translated 'alien' or 'sojourner' but is a more subtle term than either of those terms suggest. Throughout the Old Testament, *gerim* are often mentioned alongside hired hands, the poor, widows and orphans, implying that they were dependent, vulnerable members of society. Although the Jubilee legislation in Leviticus chapter 25 makes it clear that *gerim* could acquire economic stability and power, in the main the law acknowledges that they were vulnerable people and needed support in much the same way as those Israelites who had fallen out of their normal social network. In this respect, the *ger* had much in common with the asylum applicant.

The translation 'sojourner' is also misleading in as far as it implies that *gerim* were a temporary presence in Israel, whereas there is every indication that, unlike the *nokrim* and *zarim, gerim* were there to stay, and lived alongside and sometimes with the *ezrach*.

Sojourner also has faint overtones of recreation or at least intentionality, which is also misleading. The linguistic roots of the word *ger*, which include 'to stir up strife, create confusion' and 'to dread, be afraid', intimate that the presence of *gerim* was linked to social unrest or conflict, as one might expect given their implicit vulnerability.

An important distinction within the *gerim* category was the degree of their integration. The fourth commandment refers to 'the alien *[ger]* within your gates,' who is to keep the Sabbath in the same way as every other member of the household.[6] The implication of this verse, and indeed of the story of Ruth, is that individual *ger* were present within Israelite households, dealt with on a personal, one-to-one basis and hence lived by the same ethical and religious principles as their hosts. This accords with the general principle of showing hospitality to the individual *ger* that runs throughout the Torah.[7]

There is also evidence that some *gerim* did not live within and depend upon these patriarchal Israelite households. The harvest rights accorded the *ger* in

Leviticus 19.10 and 23.22 and in Deuteronomy 24.20–21 imply a degree of independence, as does the description of *gerim* as those 'who chop your wood and carry your water', in Deuteronomy 29.11, and the envisaged wealthy *ger* of Leviticus 25.47 confirms these impressions. 'Instead of requiring hospitality (as in Exodus 20.10), the "gleaning" laws appear to create a system of support that would allow those on the fringes and who were not living in Israelite households to be economically self-sufficient.'[8]

The other category of 'immigrant' is the *toshav*. Whilst it is clear that *toshav* and *ger* are sometimes used interchangeably, in Leviticus and Numbers the term *toshav* is used differently, to denote an individual who is not a community participant in the same way as a *ger* and is viewed as something of an outsider. In these two books at least, the distinction between a *ger* and a *toshav* is that between an assimilating and a non-assimilating immigrant.

Moving from our modern, if sometimes confused categories, to those used in biblical teaching is far from easy, not least because the categories themselves – *nokrim*, *zarim*, and in particular *ger* and *toshav* – cover a spectrum of positions in much the same way as 'foreigner', 'immigrant' and 'asylum seeker' do today. To get a better grasp of who these people were, we need to examine how they were treated.

The position and treatment of *gerim*

Leviticus chapter 19, verses 33–34 comprise a seminal statement concerning the position and treatment of *gerim* in Israel.

'When an alien [ger] lives with you in your land, do not ill-treat him. The alien living with you must be treated as one of your native-born. Love him as yourself, for you were aliens in Egypt. I am the LORD your God.'

The *ger* is to be protected from abuse. He or she is to be loved and treated like any *ezrach* or native person. If you need a reason it is to be found in Israel's identity – you were once aliens yourselves – which is rooted in its history, with both of these factors predicated on the fact that YHWH is their God.

This equality of treatment was not simply a nice theory that occasionally adorned Israelite ethics but ran central to the Torah and was described in considerable, concrete detail.

The *ger* and *ezrach* had equal rights before the law – 'the same law applies to the native-born and to the alien living among you'[9] – although it is more accurate to refer to the community's obligations to these individuals than their rights. Such obligations were specific and concrete. The *ger* and *ezrach* were to have equal access to justice.[10] *Gerim* were protected from abuse, oppression, economic exploitation and unfair treatment in the courts.[11] They were guaranteed the harvest gleanings,[12] fair employment practice,[13] the triennial tithe,[14] access to the cities of refuge,[15] and, latterly, even the opportunity to own rural land.[16]

Equally significantly, *gerim* were included in the feasts and praxes which were central to Israel's identity. Exodus chapter 12 gives an example of this and, in the process, outlines the principle of integration that defined participation.

The LORD said to Moses and Aaron, 'These are the regulations for the Passover: No foreigner [nokri] is to eat of it. Any slave you have bought may eat of it after you have circumcised him, but a temporary resident [toshav] and a hired worker may not eat of it … an alien [ger] living among you who wants to celebrate the Lord's Passover must have all the males in his household circumcised; then he may take part like one born in the land. No uncircumcised male may eat of it. The same law applies to the native-born [ezrach] and to the alien [ger] living among you.'[17]

The criterion for inclusion here was clearly not ethnic (both *ger* and *nokri* were technically foreigners) or economic (*ger* and hired workers would usually be of roughly equal economic standing, which was higher than that of the slave). Instead, it was circumcision – a personal sign of commitment to the covenant with God which the *ger* was free to make if he so chose. Whilst there is no indication that this was also a criterion for the legal rights outlined above, it seems that to 'belong' to Israel in a fully-fledged cultural way, the *ger* needed to express his or her commitment to the covenant which defined, shaped and directed the nation in the appropriate way. If a *ger* was willing to link his destiny to Israel, he could be integrated in this most fundamental of Israelite celebrations. If, on the other hand, he was a *toshav*, a temporary resident who had not 'thrown his lot in' with Israel, although accorded certain rights already described, he could not belong to Israel in the fullest sense of the word.

    Ger inclusion in Israel's celebrations was not limited to Passover. Deuteronomy chapter 26 describes how *gerim* were to be included in the rejoicing of first fruits, and chapter 16 says the same of the feasts of Weeks and of Tabernacles. Participation in the day of Atonement was also open to *gerim*, although probably only those who had assimilated,[18] and the same is true of the covenant ratification ceremony and the official reading of the law that are described in the closing chapters of the Torah.[19] Various verses in Leviticus and Numbers which indicate that *gerim* were allowed to make freewill offerings, fulfil vows and present burnt sacrifices, as long as they did so in the prescribed manner which *ezrach* had to follow, complete the picture of assimilating *gerim* who were full participants in the society and portray a form of inclusion which transcends that inherent in the more legalistic rights.[20]

With 'rights' came responsibilities. Enjoying the Sabbath was as much a responsibility as a right and implicit in the legislation that all had the right to rest on a Sabbath (i.e. landowners could not work family members, servants, *gerim*, or even animals non-stop) was the idea that all had the responsibility to obey this commandment. The same prohibition applied to work on the Day of Atonement and to celebrating the Feast of Unleavened Bread.[21]

More generally, the *ger* and the *ezrach* were to be treated equally in the matters of inadvertent sin,[22] 'high-handed' sin,[23] blasphemy,[24] murder, disfigurement and the killing of animals,[25] and were under the same stipulation to 'keep ... statutes and ... ordinances.'[26]

This combination of equal rights, equal prohibitions, equal punishments, and, dependent on the level of integration, equal cultic inclusion makes it very clear that *gerim* could hold a position in Israelite society which was fully integrated, although, given the reality of their situation, was still likely to be numbered among the more economically vulnerable.

The one major difference between *ger* and *ezrach* was in the ownership of land. Rural land was allocated at the time of the conquest and the Jubilee legislation meant that, in theory, it reverted to its original owners every half-century. Until the time of the return from exile, only *ezrach* could own *rural* land *in perpetuity*. Urban land and property worked differently, operating under a freehold scheme that had no restrictions on ownership and was not subject to the Jubilee legislation. *Gerim* could own property in cities in the same way as *ezrach* did.

Rural land effectively worked on a leasehold basis, rooted in the principle that in reality it belonged to God and the Israelites were merely tenants. 'The land must not be sold permanently,' God declares in Leviticus chapter 25, 'because the land is mine and you are but aliens and my tenants.' The self-identity as immigrants ran all the way into Israel's property laws. The consequence of this was that whilst *gerim* could buy, sell and own rural land (in actual fact, the reality was that they, like the native Israelites, were trading not land but usufruct), they would have to surrender it at the Jubilee.

If this seems an odd arrangement it is worth noting, in passing, the land laws that were adopted in the Ukraine after the collapse of communism that echo much of the Torah's land legislation. After an initial, equitable sharing out of land to individual parties following the demise of centralised ownership, private ownership was initially limited to Ukrainian nationals and sale-purchase of land was permitted only under very limited circumstances. Subsequent legislation relaxed these restrictions but placed a moratorium on land transactions until 2005 and thereafter, for five years, a limit of 100 hectares on private ownership.

Agricultural land could be privately owned by Ukrainian nationals (who could not permanently sell it until 2005) but not by foreigners, who, if they inherit land had to sell it within one year. Conversely, foreigners were allowed to own non-agricultural land within city limits ('in [the] case of acquiring buildings and structures and for construction purposes'), as well as non-agricultural land outside cities, ('in [the] case of acquiring structures situated on such land'). They were also entitled to participate in the privatisation of land, with the caveat that the sale of state-owned land to foreigners had to be carried out by government ministers and agreed by the Parliament, and that the sale was on condition that the foreigner registered a permanent establishment in Ukraine.[27]

This arrangement, with its fascinating balance in the ownership rights between rural and urban land, and foreign and Ukrainian nationals, was intended to protect smallholders from wealthy, external property speculators who had no connection with or loyalty to Ukraine, and in doing so to maintain national economic security and political stability. More pointedly for our purposes, it is an illuminating example of how the Israelite land laws were intended to encourage market interaction across society, without disenfranchising and alienating the native poor, fragmenting family links, and ultimately eroding and destabilising the whole society.

It is particularly interesting, therefore, to note that after the exile this legislation is reversed and the assimilated *gerim* receive a portion of the land. God tells Ezekiel:

> 'You are to distribute this land among yourselves according to the tribes of Israel. You are to allot it as an inheritance for yourselves and for the aliens who have settled among you and who have children. You are to consider them as native-born Israelites; along with you they are to be allotted an inheritance among the tribes of Israel. In whatever tribe the alien settles, there you are to give him his inheritance.'[28]

The new start which the return from exile offered Israel was analogous to that after the Exodus, when 'many other people went up with them', and subsequently became part of the nation. *Gerim*, for centuries a welcomed, vulnerable, protected and integrated section of Israelite society, became, in the long term, part of the society itself.

The position and treatment of *nokrim*

As mentioned above, *gerim*, although the most commonly mentioned and best integrated immigrants within Israelite society, were not the only foreign presence.

Nokrim were more obviously 'foreign', their presence in Israel temporary, their loyalties elsewhere and their level of integration significantly lower. The result of this was that the Israelite attitude towards them was less hospitable, and that *nokrim* were a category quite distinct from *gerim*.

These distinctions can be seen in a number of laws. Israelites were called to release one another and *gerim* from debt every seven years but not *nokrim* who were required to pay debts.[29] Similarly, whereas Israelites were not to charge interest from fellow *ezrach* or *gerim*, they could do so of *nokrim*.[30] *Nokrim* could not join the Passover feast,[31] were ineligible for kingship,[32] and were limited in their access to the assembly and to the sanctuary.[33] These restrictions point towards a clear distinction between *gerim* who were part of Israelite society but in need of economic support, and the foreigner who was outside the community and economically independent. In as far as *nokrim* were present within Israel, they appear to have been consciously foreign, autonomous and independent individuals, who had little desire to 'join' Israel.

The legislation hints at the importance of permanence and self-identification as criteria for integration, with those people whose economic, cultural and social loyalties lay elsewhere being treated differently to those who had joined Israel. The exact nature of these 'other loyalties' influenced Israelite treatment of *nokrim*. At one extreme were the Canaanites whose existence Israel was commanded to obliterate and whose practices were anathema to the nation. Time and again, it was emphasised that this brutal and draconian policy was adopted as a judgement on Canaanite culture and to protect Israel from the influence of the Canaanites' religious and cultic practices, a consideration which also lay behind the various prohibitions on intermarriage which occur in the Old Testament.[34]

Ammonites and Moabites received much the same opprobrium, although were not subject to the same genocidal programme,[35] just as the distant cities mentioned in Deuteronomy chapter 20 were offered an opportunity to surrender before battle.[36] Finally, Edomites and, perhaps surprisingly given Israel's history, Egyptians were viewed more positively still and allowed to join the cultic community from the third generation onwards.[37]

The caveat to this varied treatment of *nokrim* was that Israel was not to assume from it that they were different or chosen because they were a supremely moral or righteous people. Before the conquest of Canaan this is spelt out to them in very clear terms.

> After the LORD your God has driven them out before you, do not say to yourself, 'The LORD has brought me here to take possession of this land because of my righteousness.' No, it is on account of the wickedness of these nations that the LORD is going to drive them out before you. It is not because of your righteousness or your integrity that you are going in to take possession of their land; but on account of

> the wickedness of these nations, the LORD your God will drive them out before you ... Understand, then, that it is not because of your righteousness that the LORD your God is giving you this good land to possess, for you are a stiff-necked people.[38]

Israel's uniqueness is dependent on God's grace, a fact made painfully clear in the words of the prophet Amos. The 'national oracles' with which the book of Amos opens berate Israel for her sins alongside her neighbours, reflecting Amos's belief 'in a universal standard of conduct that conformed to and was enforced by the sovereign and universal God.'[39] Israel was different insofar as the demands placed on her were more detailed and rigorous.

Later in the same book, Amos records words that further deflate Israel's sense of superiority:

> 'Are not you Israelites
> the same to me as the Cushites?'
> declares the LORD.
> 'Did I not bring Israel up from Egypt,
> the Philistines from Caphtor
> and the Arameans from Kir?'[40]

The final comparisons strike at the very heart of Israel's sense of identity, with the Exodus being seen as simply another national migration.

Amos's words, amongst the most severe of all the prophets, underlie the tension between Israel's unique and chosen role 'to act justly ... love mercy and ... walk humbly with ... God,' by, among other things, 'loving the alien', and at the same time to 'abhor the pride' that this calling could so easily arouse.[41]

The treatment of *gerim* and *nokrim* in Old Testament Israel

It is rather more difficult to ascertain how Israel actually *did* treat its *gerim* and *nokrim* than it is to understand how it was *meant to* treat them.

The prophetic criticism which comprises so much of the Hebrew Bible covers a wide range of Israel's sins, from her idolatry and religious syncretism to her dubious foreign treaties and questionable social justice. Mixed in with these criticisms and the implications they have for Israel's *actual* as opposed to *intended* national life, there are mentions of *gerim* and *nokrim*.

When Ezekiel is called upon to indict Jerusalem around the time of the exile, he cites its violence, idolatry, social injustice, cultic and sexual impurity, and financial corruption. In amongst this woeful litany, he declares:

> 'See how each of the princes of Israel who are in you uses his power to shed blood. In you they have treated father and mother with contempt; in you they have oppressed the alien [ger] and ill-treated the fatherless and the widow.'[42]

As is so often the case, the *ger* is bracketed with those others who are socially vulnerable, 'the fatherless and the widow' and, according to Ezekiel, has been oppressed with them too. The same complaint is made a few verses later.

> 'The people of the land practise extortion and commit robbery; they oppress the poor and needy and ill-treat the alien [ger], denying them justice.'[43]

A similar accusation can be found in Jeremiah's warnings in chapters 7 and 22. In the former, the charge is religious hypocrisy: a shallow religiosity has obscured Israel's true call.

> 'Do not trust in deceptive words and say, "This is the temple of the LORD, the temple of the LORD, the temple of the LORD!" If you really change your ways and your actions and deal with each other justly, if you do not oppress the alien, the fatherless or the widow and do not shed innocent blood in this place, and if you do not follow other gods to your own harm, then I will let you live in this place, in the land I gave your forefathers for ever and ever.'[44]

Fifteen chapters later, the warning returns. *Gerim*, like orphans and widows, have been oppressed, polluting the nation and endangering its very future.

> '"This is what the LORD says: Do what is just and right. Rescue from the hand of his oppressor the one who has been robbed. Do no wrong or violence to the alien, the fatherless or the widow, and do not shed innocent blood in this place. For if you are careful to carry out these commands, then kings who sit on David's throne will come through the gates of this palace, riding in chariots and on horses, accompanied by their officials and their people. But if you do not obey these commands, declares the LORD, I swear by myself that this palace will become a ruin."'[45]

Similar warnings can be found in Zechariah[46] and Malachi[47] in which *gerim* are again bracketed with the socially vulnerable. It is, of course, impossible, to judge from these references the extent and precise nature of the 'oppression' that the prophets so railed against, but the insistent recurrence of 'the alien, the fatherless and the widow' as a social group which had been exploited in some way strongly suggests that, human nature being what it is, it was the defenceless who suffered when the people drifted from their moral and legal moorings. Old Testament Israel is an example to us not simply for showing (through its law) the way in which *gerim should* have been treated, but also for indicating (through its prophets) how they often *were* treated.

The New Testament perspective

The world changed with Jesus Christ. The extent to which his life, death and resurrection altered the role and function of Old Testament law for the believer is an interesting but immense subject and beyond the scope of this book. It is worth noting, if only in passing, that Christ's claim, made at length and with great explicitness in Matthew chapter 5, is that he had come to fulfil the law rather than abolish it.

> 'Do not think that I have come to abolish the Law or the Prophets; I have not come to abolish them but to fulfil them … whoever practises and teaches these commands will be called great in the kingdom of heaven.'[48]

Whilst it is important to balance this alongside Paul's talk about 'a righteousness from God, apart from law' and early controversies such as the need or otherwise for circumcision, it is fair to say that, however the Torah may need to be filtered through the lens of Jesus Christ, it is not to be blocked out by it.

The Torah's various political, economic and cultural stipulations were all underpinned by the basic command to 'love the alien'.[49] It was this love that made the other laws both comprehensible and possible. And it was this love – of the alien *and* of every other outcast and metaphorical alien within society – that characterised

Christ's ministry. Few issues show quite as clearly the manner in which Jesus Christ fulfilled the law.

Time and again, we hear the command to love the alien in Christ's words. When probed by an 'expert in the law' about 'eternal life', he directed the man (back) to the law and then, in response to a further question, told the story of the good Samaritan.[50] So well known to us is the story that its implications are often obscured. Hatred is not too strong a word to describe the feelings between Jews and Samaritans in the first century. On one occasion, around AD 6, according to the Jewish historian Josephus, a number of Samaritans secretly joined Jewish Passover pilgrims and entered the Temple with them. Once inside, they committed 'about the worst desecration possible' by spreading human bones in the porticoes and the sanctuary.[51] Nearly 50 years later, Samaritans from the village of Ginae murdered some Jewish pilgrims on their way to the Passover, an action which, when combined with Roman indifference in the face of calls of justice, resulted in a Jerusalem mob descending on Ginae, massacring the inhabitants and razing the village.[52] The hero of Christ's parable was not only an alien but a despised alien. The call to transcend national loyalties when faced with those in need could not have been made more provocatively.

Repeatedly in Luke's writings, Samaritans are used to explode the indifference, myopia and immorality to which nationalism can lead. Of the ten lepers healed in Luke chapter 17, the only one who returned to thank Jesus was the Samaritan.[53] Christ rebukes James and John in Luke chapter 9 for wanting to call down fire upon a Samaritan village that did not welcome them.[54] He commands the disciples in Acts chapter 1 to 'be my witnesses in Jerusalem, and in all Judea and Samaria.'[55]

Luke then proceeds to highlight the success of Philip's mission in Samaria after the Church had been persecuted following Stephen's death in Acts chapter 8 and later on describes how Paul and Barnabas heard about and then reported the success of the Church in Samaria to the council of Jerusalem.[56] The contemporary interpretation of the Torah command to love the *ger* – i.e. that the *ger* excluded Samaritans and non-resident foreigners – is systematically addressed in Luke, John and Acts.

Whilst Samaritans play the most prominent 'alien' role in the gospels, they are not alone, and it is worth mentioning in passing possibly the least prominent aliens in these books.

British people are increasingly interested in genealogies, as was seen in the overwhelming popularity of the Office for National Statistics's 1901 Census website, which had to shut down initially due to the weight of interest. Yet in spite of this, the notorious 'begat's which begin Matthew's gospel and the New Testament still leave people cold. No matter how interested we are in discovering where our family lived a century ago, we cannot comprehend the importance or seriousness that ancestry and bloodlines had to first-century Jews (or, for that matter, to most societies throughout history).

It is of some interest, therefore, that not only did Matthew include four women in Jesus' lineage, a most unusual feature for an ancient Jewish genealogy, but he included four women of very particular origins. It will be argued by some that Matthew had no choice in writing genealogies – he could not, after all, choose Jesus' lineage – but this is, of course, not true, as anyone who has noted the discrepancies between Matthew's and Luke's genealogies will acknowledge.

Instead, Jewish genealogies of the time were intended 'to establish racial purity along the lines of the model given in Ezra and Nehemiah.'[57] The fact, then, that Matthew mentions none of the well respected Jewish matriarchs, such as Sarah or Rebekah, but instead includes Tamar (v.3) and Rahab (v.5), who were Canaanites, Ruth (v.5), who was a Moabitess, and Bathsheba, whose ethnicity is not known but who was married to Uriah the Hittite, is of some significance.

Moreover, the fact that each one is mentioned in a quite unnecessary parenthesis – ' … Judah the father of Perez and Zerah, *whose mother was Tamar* … Salmon the father of Boaz, *whose mother was Rahab*, Boaz the father of Obed, *whose mother was Ruth* … David was the father of Solomon, *whose mother had been Uriah's wife*' – is surely meant to alert us to the theological point Matthew is making. In the words of one commentator, 'the inclusion of these Gentile women in the lineage would have been shocking to most Jewish readers … Matthew seems to highlight the mixed nature of Jesus's lineage purposely … [perhaps to speak] to disciples of their responsibility to cross cultural boundaries to spread Christ's gospel.'[58] Once again, in a more subtle way than Luke's recurring Samaritan stories, the limitations of national boundaries on love, compassion and the gospel are demolished.

The most explicit and moving command to love the alien comes in the parable of the sheep and goats, which Christ tells, according to Matthew, days before his rejection and death. In much the same way as the alien, orphan and widow were grouped and recognised as the vulnerable sections of Israelite society, so the 'stranger' in Matthew chapter 25 is one of those who need assistance and whose helpers will be blessed accordingly.

> 'Then the King will say to those on his right, "Come, you who are blessed by my Father; take your inheritance, the kingdom prepared for you since the creation of the world.

For I was hungry and you gave me something to eat, I was thirsty and you gave me something to drink, I was a stranger and you invited me in, I needed clothes and you clothed me, I was sick and you looked after me, I was in prison and you came to visit me."

'Then the righteous will answer him, "Lord, when did we see you hungry and feed you, or thirsty and give you something to drink? When did we see you a stranger and invite you in, or needing clothes and clothe you? When did we see you sick or in prison and go to visit you?"

'The King will reply, "I tell you the truth, whatever you did for one of the least of these brothers of mine, you did for me."'[59]

Nowhere is the New Testament's emphasis on real and practical love – on feeding, clothing, supporting, visiting, inviting in, and caring for those in need – more evident. Neither national identity nor social ostracism should stand in the way of that practical love. In the same way as the Torah placed a duty of practical love for *gerim* on the Israelites, Jesus placed one on his audience.

There is, however, one point of tension in all this. The Torah recognises a difference in the treatment of assimilating *gerim* and of non-assimilating *gerim*, and a difference between *gerim* as a whole and *nokrim*. Christ, it appears, does not. Understanding and reconciling this tension demands examining both the Torah's and Christ's respective audiences and, in doing so, investigating the other side of the argument: the host 'people' or nation in which the *gerim* or 'stranger' lives.

6. Biblical Teaching
on Nationhood

Introduction

Nationhood is a vexed issue today. Globalisation, European federalism, devolution and regionalisation have combined to question the fact of nationhood that seemed so absolute only a century ago.

Over recent years the British have become acutely conscious of the historical contingencies which forged and moulded their nation over hundreds of years. In a wider context, the fragility of the very idea of nationhood has been increasingly recognised. For much of human history, people lived in empires or tribes (or both), a division that has often been seen as synonymous with order or chaos. The nation state as we recognise it today is a 'uniquely European contribution', salvaged from the bloodstained wreckage of Christendom in the seventeenth century. Its subsequent success 'came from its achievement in concentrating power – especially the power to make and enforce the law ... in the establishment of sovereignty.'[1] It may be true that 'the package of national identity, national territory, a national army, a national economy and national democratic institutions has been immensely successful', but it is no less true that 'in a world littered with the wrecks of civilisations and empire, there is nothing particularly immortal about Great Britain or any other Western nation.'[2]

This modern tension is almost bound to colour our understanding of the biblical teaching on nationhood, making the perennial danger of quarrying Scripture for passages that buttress our existing views especially acute. In the same way as we need to make a category shift from asylum applicants and immigrants to *gerim* and *nokrim* when reading the Bible, so we need a similar shift when thinking about nations. If we try to eschew anachronistic categories when studying the biblical teaching on 'nationhood' and integration, we should hopefully avoid back-projecting our own hopes and fears onto Scripture.

The problem comes in understanding which categories *are* appropriate, and the best way of doing that is to start with the ideas which underpin nations and people groups of all kinds.

Unity and diversity

Genesis chapters 1 to 11 contain some of the most profound and influential stories in world history.

In much the same way as we have become dulled to the tale of the good Samaritan, we often hear the lyrical stories of creation, fall, flood and Babel with deaf ears. The twentieth century in particular has mired the book's opening chapters in controversy, with too many people stumbling over the fact that they were never intended to be read like a prototype scientific textbook, and so has lost sight of their profundity.

Writing of these opening chapters, Jonathan Sacks asserts simply, 'The Bible is doing here what it does elsewhere, namely conveying a set of truths through narrative.' This 'set of truths' is varied. Some are simply etiological, i.e. explaining the origins of why we wear clothes, why we dislike snakes, and so forth. Others are more profound, outlining who we are, what we are here for, what is wrong, and hinting at what the solution may be. It is these stories that provide the building blocks for the later construction of 'nationhood'.

Creation begins with one man. The Bible's first poetry is among its most momentous.

> So God created man in his own image,
> in the image of God he created him;
> male and female he created them.[3]

The interesting and endlessly-debated question over what 'his own image' entails can obscure the more fundamental fact that the text implies that as *all* human beings come from one man (or one couple) and as that first man (or couple) is made in God's image, *all* human beings therefore bear God's image. The implication of this is as far-reaching as it is disturbing.

One comment from the Mishnah, the collection of Jewish oral law written down in the third century, sums it up neatly: 'Why did God create only one human being? So that no-one can say to a fellow human being: my father was better than yours.'[4] In a similar vein, a footnote to the Churches' Commission on Racial Justice report *Asylum Voices* says, 'CCRJ works on the principle that there is only one race: the human race, but that there are different people groups, or ethnicities.' At the heart of the biblical vision lies the idea that all human beings are united in being made in God's image.

The same inevitably applies to the subsequent story of the Fall. Just as God's image marks everyone, so it is marred in everyone. Human beings are united and unified not only in their creation but also in their need for redemption 'for all have sinned and fall short of the glory of God.'[5]

Unity is not the same as uniformity, however, as we see when the camera shifts to 'a plain in Shinar' a few chapters later. Babel has often been deemed another etiological myth, intended to describe the origins of different languages (an idea which sits slightly uneasily with the 'clans and languages' of the previous chapter). While it probably does do this, it does much else besides. In some ways, the story of Babel portrays one of the foundational controversies of human history.

The story's building blocks are easily recognisable. Humanity has made a great technological leap forward in its use of bricks for stone and tar for mortar. It is united in its 'one language and common speech'. It is united in its objective to 'build ourselves a city, with a tower that reaches to the heavens.' And most importantly, it is united in its motivation, 'so that we may make a name for ourselves.' As God wryly observes, 'if as one people speaking the same language they have begun to do this, then nothing they plan to do will be impossible for them.'

The men at Shinar champion the cause that latterly became enshrined in the Enlightenment project. Mankind does not need God. Through his own commitment, effort and abilities he can achieve anything. Utopia is one building project away.

This view remains popular today despite the fact that the fruit it bore in the twentieth century was unimaginably bitter. As Jonathan Glover pithily remarks in his moral history of the twentieth century, 'communism, the major sustained attempt to put an extreme version of the Enlightenment outlook into practice, was a human catastrophe.'[6]

It is the recognition of this that informs the rather different biblical view. One nineteeth century rabbi commenting on Genesis chapter 11 interpreted Babel as the first totalitarianism and Jonathan Sacks, expanding on this, writes, '[Babel] is a supreme act of hubris … it is the attempt to impose an artificial unity on divinely created diversity.'[7] God's intervention at Shinar is not simply a device to explain linguistic variety or even a way of putting mankind in his place, but of affirming what Sacks calls 'the dignity of difference'.

> God, the creator of humanity, having made a covenant [the Noahide] with all humanity, then turns to one people and commands it to be different, *teaching humanity to make space for difference. God may at times be found in human other, the one not like us… the unity of God is to be found in the diversity of creation.* [italics original][8]

Babel is a turning point in the biblical story, with subsequent verses focusing down onto Abraham, at which point the nature and tone of the narrative change. From the archetypes of Genesis 1–11, we move to a specific named individual, together with his family and his personal situation.

The bigger vision is never lost, though, and indeed becomes a foundation of the 'particularity' which Abraham's call represents. God's plan and the biblical narrative may now rest on the shoulders of a single man, family and latterly people, but it is still firmly rooted in a worldwide vision. God's promise is *to* Abraham but *for* 'all peoples'.

> 'I will make you into a great nation and I will bless you;
> I will make your name great, and you will be a blessing.

I will bless those who bless you, and whoever curses you I
will curse;
and all peoples on earth will be blessed through you.'[9]

In this way the entire biblical story begins with an
oscillation, tension and tentative resolution between
unity and diversity. Unity is not the same as uniformity.
Diversity is not the same as anarchy. It is upon these
foundations that the biblical idea of nationhood is built.

Biblical 'nations'

Israel was conceived among, born under, surrounded by,
and eventually exiled into foreign 'nations'. The early
Church spread through the Roman Empire with
astonishing rapidity and within decades had reached
most of the empire's major cities. One cannot read the
Bible without having a sense of the wider geopolitical
picture.

This wealth of information is a double-edged sword,
however, as much of it simply portrays the contemporary
situation and even then only inasmuch as it impinged on
Israel or the Church. When looking at biblical 'nations' it
is important to disentangle normative biblical teaching
from narrative biblical description.

The 'nations' that are mentioned in the Bible's pages
are hugely varied. At one end of the scale there are the
empires of Egypt, Assyria, Babylonia, Persia and Rome.
These 'nations' lasted centuries, encompassed huge
geographical areas and incorporated a wide variety of
people groups. They imposed order and cultural unity to
different degrees and treated subject peoples differently,
according to their strength, wealth, importance and
attitude.

At the other end of the scale, Amos's 'oracle against the nations' in the opening chapters of his prophecy, includes rebukes of Gaza and Tyre, Philistine and Phoenician city-states respectively, alongside more obvious 'nations' such as Edom and Moab. This inclusiveness suggests that while the biblical narrative recognises mankind's propensity to form and operate self-governing groups or communities (for which he will be held accountable), there is no pattern for what these groups might look like.

The biblical attitude to 'nations' tends to hinge not so much on the nature of their political organisation but on their attitude to Israel or the Church, their social justice, and their religious, cultural and moral behaviour. Insofar as political organisation influences these categories, it would be possible to detect a normative model in biblical teaching, but the fact that the 'nations' which earn most opprobrium – the Canaanite city states in the Hexateuch and Rome in Revelation – have next to nothing in common in terms of size and order strongly suggests that it is the *values* of the 'national' community rather than its size or precise political constitution that are ultimately important.

To this basic observation – that biblical 'nations' come in all shapes and sizes, and are approved or condemned according to their values and behaviour rather than their constitution – we can add three relevant points.

The first is that Genesis chapters 1–9 are notable for their silence on nationality. Karl Barth pointed out that nationhood does not appear in these crucial early chapters and, as such, he was unwilling 'to grant nation-hood the status of "an order of creation"'.[10] Arguments from silence are notoriously weak, but considering what could have been said about national identities and differences in these chapters, and what is said about humanity's identity and unity, Barth is surely right to recognise that these chapters contain nothing to suggest that national borders or the make-up of people groups is sacrosanct.

Second, and more substantively, the story of Pentecost in Acts chapter 2 apparently enacts a reversal of the story of Babel. Having been divided *into* and then *by* their separate tongues at Shinar, people 'from every nation under heaven' are brought together to hear the apostles' new message in Jerusalem.

Whilst largely true, this reading omits one important detail that shows how Babel is not quite reversed at Pentecost. As the narrative of Acts makes quite clear, the linguistic diversity of the Parthians, Medes and the other peoples was not abolished and replaced by 'one tongue' in Jerusalem but merely and temporarily overcome. At Pentecost diversity is transcended not eradicated. In much the same way, Paul would later assert that he was an 'Israelite … a descendant of Abraham, from the tribe of Benjamin,' and a 'Roman citizen', while at the same time acknowledging that 'everything [is] a loss compared to the surpassing greatness of knowing Christ Jesus my Lord'. [11]

Third, the vision of the book of Revelation demonstrates a similar appreciation of difference.[12] Revelation draws on the opening chapters of Genesis in many different ways and one of these is the fourfold formula used for describing the people of the world in Genesis chapter 10: families, languages, lands and nations. Time and again, John uses these four terms – or, more precisely, the Greek terms used for them in the Septuagint: *phyle*, *glossa*, *chora*, and *ethne* – to describe his vision. The people who stand before the throne at the end of time have not had all traces of their unique identities drained from them. The great multitude may be countless but it is not characterless.

At the same time, it is worth noting that this fourfold formula occurs a total of seven times throughout the vision, in a different order on each occasion.[13] In the book of Revelation numbers are never accidental.

> In Revelation, four is the number of the world, seven the number of completeness. The sevenfold use of this fourfold phrase indicates that reference is being made to all the nations of the world. In the symbolic world of Revelation, there could hardly be a more emphatic indication of universalism.[14]

Neither Genesis nor Pentecost nor Revelation demand nationhood or legitimise nationalism. Nevertheless, together they provide a counterpoint to the fluid concept of nationhood that runs throughout the biblical story. If mankind is a relational animal, communities, people groups and nations are natural, i.e. created phenomena, and the characteristics that these lend to individuals add colour and 'dignity' to creation.[15] Diversity is never licence for segregation, xenophobia or isolationism – no matter what ethnicity we are, we are still members of the same race – but it is reason to question political and cultural imperialism and scrutinise plans that involve the abolition of national borders.

Israel and nationhood

Studying the Bible's 'nations' can only take us so far. Biblical authors tended only to be interested in other nations insofar as they interacted with Israel or the nascent Church, and details of their internal dynamics, land, language, family, government, religion and culture are sparse.

The only nation which is explored in any detail is, of course, Israel itself and it is to Israel that we must turn to get an understanding of how the nation reacted to the presence of immigrants.

In doing so, an important caveat must be made. Looking to Israel to understand the balance between 'nation' and 'immigrant' does not oblige us to imitate Israel exactly. By any measure, biblical Israel was a unique case and many of its defining characteristics were rightly inherited by the Church rather than by particular, historically contingent nation states. The tendency of some Protestant nations to view themselves as the 'new Israel' or of certain Orthodox Churches to hitch their creed and culture to an ethnic nationalism (a heresy known as phyletism and condemned by an Orthodox council of 1872 but subsequently largely ignored) is distinctly unhealthy.[16] Israel's unique call to 'love the Lord your God with all your heart and with all your soul and with all your strength' is matched by no nation in history, and certainly none today. The nation's distinctive religious definition and allegiance needs to be remembered particularly if we wish to avoid the trap of seeing religious allegiance as a basis of nationality.

This warning in place, Israel's nationhood can be examined and a number of defining points seen. The first is that the nation of Israel was based on a distinct historical, cultural and creedal identity. While this might well be called a 'religious' identity, the word can be misleading, carrying with it post-Enlightenment ideas of religion as personal spirituality. Israel's identity was far more public and all encompassing than that.

Whereas Roman citizenship primarily exempted you from degrading punishment and gave you the right to a public trial, to be an Israelite was to have a particular and public identity and worldview, which can be seen in a number of ways.[17]

It was first and foremost based on a number of fundamental beliefs that shaped the Israelite mind and society: monotheism, creation, election, covenant and redemption. It was expressed through a number of stories that were the flesh on the bones of these basic beliefs: of Abraham and election, of Jacob and descent into Egypt, of Moses and liberation from slavery, of Joshua and the conquest of Canaan, of David and the golden age of kingship, of Ezra and Nehemiah and the return from exile, and latterly of Judas Maccabaeus and the eviction of gentile tyranny.

It was enacted in the yearly round of celebrations and festivals, which united seminal moments of Israel's history with agricultural harvests. Passover celebrated the Exodus with the barley harvest, Pentecost celebrated the giving of Torah on Sinai with the wheat harvest and the bringing of first fruits to the Temple, and Tabernacles celebrated the wilderness wandering on the way to Canaan with the grape harvest. These three festivals retold Israel's story, implicit in which were the nation's beliefs, and more importantly invited men, women, children and *gerim* to *participate in the retelling*. Subsequently, two other festivals, Hannukah and Purim, performed a similar function, celebrating the overthrow of Antiochus Epiphanes by Judas Maccabaeus and the reversal of Haman's plot to destroy the Jews in the Persian empire, respectively.

The nation's identity and worldview were also embodied in the symbols that dominated the Israelite mindset, landscape and daily life. Jerusalem and the Temple were 'the focal point[s] of every aspect of Jewish national life', being the nation's religious, national and political headquarters, not to mention the place where God was supposed to dwell with his people. [18] The Torah was God's loving commands to his people, sanctioning and regulating Temple activity, structuring social and personal life, being discussed and observed by individuals every day, and attaining particular importance during the deprivation of exile. The Sabbath, the Sabbath year, the Jubilee, circumcision and food laws all represented aspects of Israelite identity and worldview in some way.

It was also seen in the distinct moral lifestyle of the people. The law we read in the Pentateuch was to be read and inwardly digested by everyone, at all times and in all places, as Deuteronomy chapter 6 makes clear.[19] Nor was it just a device to shape the Israelite mind but instead was the basis of all personal, national, economic and social life – to be lived rather than just read – and not as an exercise in moral gymnastics but, as the Israelites are repeatedly told, 'so that it may go well with you', and so that nations 'who will hear about all these decrees [will] say, "Surely this great nation is a wise and understanding people."'[20]

From this (by no means exhaustive) list of beliefs, stories, ceremonies, symbols and lifestyle it should be clear that belonging to the nation of Israel meant far more than being able to exercise certain political rights. For Israel nationhood was a matter of belonging to *and participating in* a 'narrative community', with this particular narrative offering being nothing less than a comprehensive, multi-layered answer to the most basic questions of human life: who am I? (identity), where am I going? (destiny), and what am I here for? (purpose).

Paradoxically, the 'political' structure that we might more naturally see as a foundation of nationhood was less important to Israel, although this is not to suggest that 'politics' was irrelevant. The Torah sets out a multipolar, non-hierarchical structure through which the nation was governed.[21] Individual, family, community, tribe, Levites and the nation each acted as separate sources of authority, with its own geographic and legal areas of jurisdiction, each group dealing with those issues most appropriate to them. The king himself was regulated to quite an astonishing degree compared to the quasi-divine status of contemporary monarchs.

> The king, moreover, must not acquire great numbers of horses for himself or make the people return to Egypt to get more of them... He must not take many wives, or his heart will be led astray. He must not accumulate large amounts of silver and gold... [he must] not consider himself better than his brothers.[22]

The constitution was set up in such a way as to foster 'political' participation without transferring loyalty or the sense of belonging from the covenant to particular kings or institutions. Israel was to remain God's people – a nation united through a collective story into which immigrants could assimilate if they so chose.

Israel's attitude to and expression of nationhood hence differed subtly from our modern conceptions. Less emphasis was placed on political sovereignty and jurisdiction and more on a common sense of purpose and belonging. The nation of Israel was consciously a narrative and 'imagined' community.

These senses of purpose and of belonging were rooted firmly in the nation's foundational 'religious' beliefs. As the frequent tawdry interludes in the nation's history testify, neither was a foolproof deterrent against internal conflict and strife in the way a more absolutist or authoritarian regime might have been.

On the other hand, this model did enable the nation to preserve its population and identity with extraordinary tenacity though a prolonged period of transition and international conflict, whilst maintaining an open welcome to vulnerable immigrants and without descending into ethnic isolationism.

Israel: nationhood and ethnicity

As observed in the previous chapter, Israel had an open attitude towards *gerim* who were prepared to assimilate into the culture. With the exception of kingship (which was limited to *ezrach*) and permanent possession of rural land (at least until the return from exile), *gerim* were full and equal members of Israelite society. Israel's borders were permeable to people but not, in theory, to values.

This, combined with the detail in Exodus that 'many other people went up with [Israel]' to escape Egypt and start a new life, suggests that ethnicity was not a prerequisite of nationhood in Israel, at least at first.[23] To belong to Israel was a matter of will not simply of birth.

The major exception to this came in the wake of the exile. The opening chapters of 1 Chronicles and the books of Ezra and Nehemiah testify to an urgent, and to us unpalatable, desire to demonstrate and maintain 'ethnic purity' in Israel. The long genealogies which appear in each of the three books 'bear witness to the strongly felt need in the newly founded community to make good its claim to be the children of Abraham, Isaac and Jacob.'[24] Ezra in particular shows great hostility towards intermarriage, with the narrator reacting furiously when leaders come to him and say that 'the people of Israel… have not kept themselves separate from the neighbouring peoples with their detestable practices.'

> 'We have disregarded the commands you gave through your servants the prophets when you said: "The land you are entering to possess is a land polluted by the corruption

of its peoples. By their detestable practices they have filled it with their impurity from one end to the other. Therefore, do not give your daughters in marriage to their sons or take their daughters for your sons. Do not seek a treaty of friendship with them at any time, that you may be strong and eat the good things of the land and leave it to your children as an everlasting inheritance."'[25]

Ezra's lament leads to a national confession, series of divorces and an attitude of isolationism. The book of Nehemiah records a similar stance of segregation, in which the Israelites 'separated themselves from the neighbouring peoples for the sake of the Law of God.'[26] The people vow 'not to give our daughters in marriage to the peoples around us or take their daughters for our sons,' in the same way as they vow to observe festivals, cancel debts every seven years and not to trade on the Sabbath.

This ethnic isolationism appears to contradict the thrust of the Torah until its precise context is understood. The sense of revival that marked the return from Babylon was intimately bound up with repentance for past sins and the resolution not to repeat history. Time and again, the ethnic separation that appears in Ezra and Nehemiah has nothing to do with the ethnicity of Israel's neighbours' and everything to do with their morality.

Both Ezra and Nehemiah seem to be saying that earlier intermarriages in Israel's history led to the apostasy that resulted in exile. They are horrified that Israel is falling into the same pattern again... [and] cast the danger of intermarriage with foreigners as one of apostasy driven by the pagan beliefs of the foreign spouse. Ethnic or racial issues, other than religion, are not at all related to the prohibition.[27]

'Foreigners' in this immediate post-exilic period epitomise the sinful foreign practices into which the Israelites slid before, thus precipitating the exile. It is for this reason that the prohibitions against intermarriage are linked with denunciations of 'detestable practices' or contextualised alongside other cultural and moral issues, such as trading on the Sabbath. It is this reinvigorated desire to remain morally and culturally pure, combined with the returned nation's innate vulnerability amidst the regional anti-Semitism evident in Esther, which motivated this seemingly anomalous ethnic isolationism, which had hardened to aggressive nationalism by the time of Jesus.

New Testament nationhood

The Jewish historian Josephus wrote for a Roman audience as an apologist for his people. He was eager to make first-century Jews appear as accommodating and hospitable to pagans and pagan ideas as he could. Yet even he recognised that the first-century Israelite welcome only went so far.

> To all who desire to come and live under the same laws with us, he [i.e. Moses] gives a gracious welcome, holding that it is not family ties alone which constitute relationship, but agreement in the principles of conduct. On the other hand, it was not his pleasure that casual visitors should be admitted to the intimacies of our daily life.[28]

In reality, by the time Josephus was writing, this division was somewhat hopeful, with Jewish nationalism being an immensely complex phenomenon. The Roman occupation provoked a spectrum of reactions, ranging from collaboration through complete segregation to active rebellion. Rome made Judea a province in its own right in the early years of the first century but the 'succession of "prefects" or "procurators" [who] governed with more or less crass folly' meant that tension remained high.[29]

It is within this context of occupation, tension and confused and sometimes highly aggressive nationalism that Jesus' teachings need to be seen. His ministry was, as observed, the archetype of inclusiveness. He invited the nation's social outcasts and, on the occasions he encountered them, foreigners to take their place alongside 'orthodox' Jews at the banquet of the Father. Time and again, Christ's example and stories of love and forgiveness transcend all social and national boundaries.

Transcending social and national boundaries did not entail ignoring those that were moral or 'religious', however. John's account of Christ's conversation with the Samaritan woman in chapter 4 of his gospel illustrates this well.[30] The woman is astounded that Jesus is not troubled by her sex or nationality. 'You are a Jew and I am a Samaritan woman. How can you ask me for a drink?' she asks, with the narrator helpfully interjecting, 'For Jews do not associate with Samaritans.' Ignoring such cultural boundaries did not prevent Jesus from criticising her marital ethics or asserting the 'superiority of the Jewish understanding of God,' however.[31] 'You Samaritans worship what you do not know; we worship what we do know, for salvation is from the Jews.'

In reality, Christ did not see this balance of openness and truthfulness as a major break with the past. He was clear about his role as fulfilment of the law, and stated, in a faint echo of Deuteronomy 4.6–8, that he wanted his disciples to live in such a way as to 'let your light shine before men, that they may see your good deeds and praise your Father in heaven.'[32]

And yet, the fact that Christ was the *fulfilment* of the law meant that the story was now different. The disciples became the quorum of a new narrative community, their story being the old one with a decisive new climax and point of departure.

The major change in terms of nationhood was that this new narrative now moved beyond the political and cultural confines of the old story. The Kingdom of God bypassed the traditional symbols and praxes of faith that had marked Israel as a distinct nation. Jesus himself assumed the identity of Israel. He became the climax of the covenant, the new Temple, the final sacrifice, and the perfect, distinct, moral life. More pointedly, he was Israel's true king whose kingdom was 'from another place' and knew no boundaries.[33]

The historic boundaries of the narrative community that was Israel were exploded in the great commission and the Church became an international 'nation' whose borders were ethical, creedal and baptismal, and whose king demanded his people's ultimate loyalty. Once Peter had the vision which abolished the food laws in Acts 10 and the debate over circumcision had been won by Paul in Acts 15, baptism was the only formal prerequisite for joining and belonging to the new 'nation of faith', and membership was through faith alone.

Calling the Church a 'nation' in this way may sound like a violation of the word, yet it is an analogy with some precedent in the New Testament. Peter described the churches to whom he wrote as 'a holy nation'.[34] Paul told the Philippians that their citizenship was in heaven.[35] The book of Hebrews describes the examples of faith as 'aliens and strangers on earth' who were 'looking for a country of their own... a better country – a heavenly one.'[36] And Revelation has the city of New Jerusalem indicating the believers' true citizenship.[37]

This new nationality was fundamental to the vision of the kingdom and took precedence over other identities: whoever or wherever one was, being 'in Christ' was what counted. It did not abolish them, however. Paul still paraded his Jewish heritage, frequently cited his Roman citizenship and happily claimed its privileges. He was willing to use cultural distinctiveness as a vehicle for his work.[38] He made it clear that Jews and Greeks remained Jews and Greeks, and men and women remained men and women. The difference now was that these cultural distinctions were not to act as boundaries to those who were 'in Christ'. Love of the Messiah made all other loyalties fade into insignificance.

Conclusion

The New Testament takes the particular 'national' identity of Israel and, through Christ, transforms it into the particular 'national' identity of the Church. Neither is an exact model for modern nations but both provide examples of what nations should and shouldn't be.

The nation of Israel was a 'narrative community' *par excellence*, its unique identity surviving the most remarkable injuries, some geopolitical, some self-inflicted. Its combination of faith, history, worldview, practices, festivals, constitution and lifestyle enabled it to foster participation, maintain open boundaries, welcome foreigners, protect the vulnerable, and preserve its values over a millennium, admittedly with varying degrees of success.

The Church took this model and extended it across the face of the globe. Loyalty to Christ as king supplants all other national loyalties, preventing any other narrative community from claiming the individual's ultimate devotion. Cultural distinctiveness is maintained and celebrated even to the end of time but never allowed to be the defining characteristic of a people.

As William Temple remarked centuries years later, at a time of desperate national crisis and in an era of fevered nationalism:

> When we turn to prayer it could not be as Britons who happened to be Christians; it must be as Christians who happened to be British. Otherwise we fall into the error of our enemies, whose distinctive sin it was that they put their nationality first.[39]

7. Principles, Policies and Practice

Introduction

The task of translating biblical teaching into governing principles and public policy has a long, detailed, complex and controversial history, which could fill a book ten times this size.[1]

At its most basic, the exercise involves a two-stage process of de- and re-contextualisation. The intentions and principles behind specific teachings must first be derived from their contexts before being applied to contemporary situations, the alternative being painfully anachronistic government. There is usually a reasonable degree of unanimity over the first of these stages, although a number of caveats must be recognised. Biblical teaching should not be cherry-picked to suit existing agendas. Attention must be paid to Israel's unique covenantal status. All Scripture, particularly the Old Testament, must be read through the lens of Jesus Christ. With such caveats in place, the process of deriving principles from texts, whilst never easy, is at least possible.

More problematically, there will almost always be disagreement about the second stage in the process, in much the same way as there is uncertainty when principles are translated into policies in any area. Principles are value-based, goal-oriented propositions. Policies, on the other hand, are methods that are deeply embedded in and influenced by social, cultural and economic conditions. Theology cannot unilaterally dictate specific policies and 'the Church acting corporately should not commit itself to any particular policy' which, in William Temple's words, will 'always depend on technical decisions concerning the actual relations of cause and effect in the political and economic world.'[2]

For this reason, this chapter is split into two parts. The first examines the relevant principles from the biblical teaching reviewed in chapters 5–7, whilst the second tentatively explores how these might be translated into policy and practice.

Principles

There are, perhaps, ten overarching principles relevant to the issues of asylum and immigration today that might be derived from the biblical teaching, many of which exist in tension with other principles.

1. The unity of mankind

We are, in the words of the Churches' Commission on Racial Justice, 'only one race', divided as that may be into 'different people groups or ethnicities'. My brother is my brother, irrespective of distance, skin colour or culture. Our neighbours are not just those with whom we share things in common but despised 'Samaritans' too. Any attitude or policy that disregards this or assumes ontological divisions within humanity is unacceptable.

The implications of this should be obvious. All forms of race politics are unacceptable. Public rhetoric that alienates 'the other' because they are other is unacceptable. Public policy that dehumanises 'the other' for the same reason is likewise intolerable.

2. The reality of nationhood

At the same time, there is a reality to nationhood that extends beyond mere chance and circumstance. Humans are relational beings and gathered communities (perhaps a better term than the loaded word 'nation') are genuine entities, in the sense of being deliberate, narrative groups, responsible and accountable for their decisions. In the same way, borders may be historically contingent but are nonetheless real, simply because the communities they define are real.

This is not, of course, the same as saying that modern nations must be preserved at all costs or that borders are immutable or impermeable. Borders and communities change with circumstance. It is, however, to claim that the existence and borders of people groups are not to be ignored as wholly arbitrary and immaterial and that, accordingly, governments and people have a right to safeguard them and maintain the nation's narrative community.

3. National borders: permeable to people but not values

Israel's borders were open to people rather more than they were to values. Whilst this is a clear principle in theory, in practice the extent to which it is specific to Israel is debatable.

In one respect, Israel had no choice in the matter. Secure borders are an anachronistic concept for an ancient Near East society. Moreover, Israel's passionate protection of her beliefs and value system surely reflects the nation's unique role and status, and cannot be translated across centuries and continents.

The desire to imitate this particular principle may, therefore, be somewhat misguided. The sentiments expressed by one interviewee in Yasmin Alibhai-Brown's book, *Who do we think we are?*, the daughter of an Indian couple who arrived in Britain in the 1950s, are enough to warn us of the folly of protecting certain national values simply because they are *ours*.

> 'My parents' generation were completely uncritical of Great Britain as they call it. People like me are the opposite because we have grown up here and we see through their façade. They carry on destroying the world. I see them drowning in drugs, divorce and depression. I see them unable to control their children. I see them producing filth and violence and claiming it is some kind of freedom. I see love between men and women evaporating... Why should I take this road in the name of progress?'[3]

An uncritical preservation of a culture's values is tantamount to blind nationalism, against which the Israelites were frequently warned.[4]

That said there is an element within this principle that suggests that a nation needs some mutually agreed idea of what it stands for in order to foster a sense of belonging, and that it is legitimate to wish to protect and maintain that identity. Modern national values, unlike Israel's, are not to be maintained at all costs, but this does not mean they should be abandoned in the face of major immigration or other large-scale culture shifts.

4. 'Loving the alien'

Within the context of these three broad-brush principles – the unity of mankind, the reality of 'nations', and the importance of 'national' values – there are a number of others that focus specifically on the role and position of the immigrant.

The oft-repeated command for Israel and Christ's followers to love the alien is the immovable object within the whole debate. As we have seen, this 'love' is not meant in the vague, warm, well-meaning sense of 'being nice', as it is so often used today, but rather as the basis of a hard-nosed call to ensure social, moral, economic and relational well-being and justice. Such concrete manifestations of this underlying principle will be examined below, but it is worth treating this over-arching command as a principle in itself.

As a principle, loving the alien demands not only social and economic justice but also a measured, positive tone in public discourse, which eschews crass generalisations, aggressive polemic and hostility. If we are to love the alien, we must avoid slipping into a tone of wearied tolerance or open resentment whenever we talk about him or her.

This is not, it must be emphasised, the same as going to the other extreme and denying the right to talk about illegal immigration, criminal activity amongst asylum applicants or 'NHS tourism', simply for fear of demonising immigrants. Such wilful blindness does no one any good.

Rather, it is a call to set a constructive tone for the debate, to shun deliberately incendiary metaphors and examples, and to avoid blaming the majority of 'aliens' for the sins of a few.

5. *The rights of immigrants*

The primary way in which the command to love the alien assumed flesh was in *gerim*'s basic 'rights' or, more accurately, the basic responsibilities that Israelites had towards *gerim*.

Irrespective of their level of integration, *gerim* had equal rights before the law. They were protected from abuse, oppression, economic exploitation and unfair treatment in the courts. Those who had chosen not to assimilate may not have been entitled to participate in national feasts but they were accorded economic, employment and legal rights nonetheless.

Although the precise way in which these translate into the contemporary world will vary according to the legal and economic particularities of different societies, the overall implications of equality in terms of policing, law, employment policy and access to welfare should be clear.

6. *The responsibilities of immigrants*

In the same way as *gerim* had equal 'rights' before the law, they also faced equal prohibitions and equal punishments. To love someone is not to tolerate everything they do, to excuse their bad behaviour or to avoid setting any restrictions or regulations upon their freedom. Love is not the same as liberty.

Although this may sound obvious, our modern rights-based culture, with its inclination towards omni-tolerance and pardoning behaviour because of circumstance, can often forget that without responsibility or any coherent concept of moral interdependence, rights can never be realised. If immigrants are entitled to the rights of the law, they are also obliged to accept its responsibilities, and indeed to respect its culture, traditions and social conventions.

7. *A willingness to integrate*

Over and above the primary level of basic 'rights', *gerim* could be included, *if they so chose*, in the feasts and praxes which were central to Israel's identity. In other words, the option of full cultural integration was open to them.

This was most apparent in circumcision, the clearest and most important sign that the *ger* had thrown his lot in with the host nation. Refusal to integrate could not to be used as an excuse to mistreat or dehumanise the immigrant, as noted above, but a comprehensive sense of belonging was only open to those who had expressed their allegiance to the nation and its key values.

The implications of this principle are as clear as they are controversial. Optional graduated integration has not been a popular policy in Britain over recent decades, yet the covenantal basis of Israel's life, seen here in the importance of deliberate, personal commitment of the individual to the community (and, below, of the community to the individual) points in that direction.

While recognising this, we also need to face the important question of whether optional, graduated integration, which includes some public act of personal commitment, such as Israel's circumcision or the citizenship ceremonies that are treated so seriously in many nations, can be forced upon immigrants without native-born residents being asked to make the same commitment. Is it right to ask immigrants to accept responsibilities and a cultural identity in a way that many natives are not willing to?

8. *A willingness to accept integration*

The implicit, optional, graduated integration of *gerim* within the Torah is matched by the many responsibilities laid on Israelites to accept and accommodate the stranger in their midst. It is not acceptable to call for integration from the immigrant without meeting him or her 'half way'. Integration was not something that was to happen grudgingly, for either party.

This can be seen today in the often elaborate and emotional citizenship ceremonies in a number of countries, such as Canada, the United States and Australia. It is also in marked contrast to the, until recently, wholly unceremonious, largely personal, all-but silent process in the UK.

There are also implications here for the nature of local and national political leadership and for media ethics, as well as for the basic concept of citizenship. Strong leadership and constructive media attitudes are all needed to foster positive attitudes to immigration. The effect of headlines, such as the *Evening Standard*'s famous front page on the day the Empire Windrush docked in 1948, which read 'Welcome Home', cannot be under-estimated.

9. Compassion for the vulnerable

Beyond these five principles concerning the respective rights and responsibilities of immigrants and host nations, there are two additional principles that, whilst not focused specifically on *gerim* or *ezrach*, are highly relevant to the overall debate. The first of these is the imperative of compassion for the vulnerable.

Gerim are continually associated with widows and orphans, the implication being that they were among the most vulnerable members of society. The nation earns strong condemnation for its mistreatment of the vulnerable, this being one of the critical litmus tests of its social health.

There are several possible implications of this principle. One is that a nation should be proud rather than grudging in its acceptance of the truly vulnerable. There are few higher callings than to clothe the naked, feed the hungry and house the homeless.

Second, however, there is the reminder that immigrants are, in one respect, no different to the widows and fatherless. There is no warrant to prioritise one needy group over another and if a particularly vulnerable, native-born, socio-economic group is being ignored for the sake of another, something is wrong. Decisions to accept and house successful asylum applicants should be seen as a triumph of love over rejection. However, when such decisions are taken by the wealthy and comfortable yet involve housing asylum applicants in 'communities' that are socially and economically depressed, power is not being used as it should, and localised tension becomes understandable.

10. The Church as the model of a cross-cultural community

A final relevant principle comes in the role of the Church.

The Church should transcend all national borders and act as the model for an international community. It should be prepared to challenge government policy if that policy flouts gospel principles. It should exemplify the welcome and hospitality and humanising attitude to the stranger that Christ so powerfully speaks of in Matthew 25. It should, in short, be the model of an international, inter-ethnic, locally active, belonging community.

Exactly what this entails will be debatable. In one sense, it is clear, as the practical examples below illustrate. In another, it is difficult, presenting questions such as, do we, as Christians, have a greater loyalty to fellow believers who come seeking asylum than to non-believers?

The answer to this question, as to other equally specific ones will depend on a range of indeterminate issues. It is, as we have observed, extremely difficult to declare that this particular principle demands this particular policy as there is rarely an obvious link between the two: policies are invariably too specific and circumstantially contingent to be *proved* the *necessary* consequence of a general principle. Nevertheless, it is to policies we now turn, in an attempt to sketch out what a biblical approach to asylum and immigration might look like.

Policies

Principles may not be able to dictate policies but they can guide and veto them.

An example of this can be seen in the asylum voucher scheme that was abandoned in the wake of much criticism in April 2002. This provided asylum applicants with vouchers instead of cash that they could exchange at designated shops for food and clothing. With the (not inconsiderable) benefit of hindsight, it can be seen that whilst the policy may have had the acceptable objective of acting as a disincentive to false claimants, it ultimately fell outside the bounds permitted by the principles outlined above, partly because it alienated the users and marked them off from the rest of society, and partly because it actively impoverished them (change was not given for voucher transactions, hence forcing asylum applicants to pay inflated prices for basic goods).

In this fashion, the principles outlined above can act as 'boundary conditions' for policy initiatives, not so much insisting on what *must* be done but indicating what *should not* – a pattern which reflects the natural mechanism of much of the Torah itself, in which many commands tell Israel what they should not do, rather than what they should. Having said this, 'boundary conditions' implicitly offers guidance on what should be done and there is no reason why this implicit guidance cannot become explicit in certain circumstances.

What follows is a series of thoughts which are shaped by this dual 'veto and guidance' function, but also by the awareness that policies are by their nature detailed, short term, numerous, and circumstantial. To analyse all asylum and immigration policies in this way would require a substantial book rather than part of one chapter and would almost certainly be out of date before publication. Instead, this chapter offers a brief analysis of the more substantive areas of policy, corresponding to the contours of the debates outlined in chapter 2 and 3.

Domestic asylum policy

The fundamental tension in asylum policy is, as we have seen, between the moral imperative of welcoming the vulnerable and the judicial imperative of securing borders against the dishonest.

The insistent and repeated emphasis on loving the alien, with everything that entailed, throughout the entire biblical canon warns us that it is the first part of this tension – the mercy and humanity – which must be our guiding light. It is better to err on the side of love and risk exploitation by the unscrupulous, than to err on the side of inflexible legality and risk the further de-humanisation of the weak and vulnerable.

This will mean, at a general level, that there should be strong leadership and positive rhetoric with an emphasis not so much on the benefits that asylum applicants bring – they are, after all, not accepted on the basis of their economic potential – but rather on the moral case for asylum. If how we treat others is fundamental to how we define ourselves, and how we treat the vulnerable is particularly important in God's eyes, a nation that willingly accepts those who are fleeing from a genuine risk of persecution should be proud that it does so. The privatisation of morality in the modern West has made it difficult to base political decisions on moral arguments like these, but if there were ever a case for that to be reversed, it is here.

This should also have implications for the tone and level of the debate in the public sphere. Newspapers are self-regulating and accountable primarily to proprietors or shareholders and thus can often get away with rhetoric which would be quite unacceptable were it to come from a politician or major public figure. Yet, in spite of protests to the contrary, the opinion-forming power of the media is quite unrivalled.

Press regulation is an awkward and unappealing option, yet the consistent and successful demonisation of asylum applicants in some widely read quarters is unhelpful, poisoning the wells of public discourse and turning public opinion against an already vulnerable group of people. In the light of the current wave of anti-discriminatory legislation, the hostility towards asylum applicants encouraged by certain headlines is worthy of official attention. In our society's welcome desire to protect minority groups from public prejudice, surely asylum applicants constitute one such vulnerable group?

In terms of the asylum application process itself, our eagerness for an efficient system free from backlog should not allow corners to be cut. Translators and legal advice need to be of appropriate standard (as some reports suggest they have not been) and allowances must be made for the educational and intellectual level of applicants.

During the intermediary stage, there is good cause to suggest that asylum applicants should be kept within the state's orbit. Both for the sake of genuine asylum applicants who would otherwise be sucked into the shadowy world of pending applications, and disingenuous ones who may use the delay in process to 'disappear', there should be close control of applicants at this stage.

There is much to recommend the use of accommodation centres for this purpose *if, and only if,* they can be shown to be secure and speed up the process, to protect the vulnerable, and to act as an effective deterrent to false claimants. The processing of applicants and applications abroad, as suggested by the Conservative Party and practised in Australia, has the same objective with the advantage of relieving pressure on UK resources. However, the practical considerations of this, given the intense land usage in virtually every nearby country, not to mention the moral shadows of the policy – alienation and deportation – do not recommend it. A third option, that of tagging applicants, is unacceptable, as is accommodating them in prisons or other unsuitable centres.

Successful asylum applicants need to be settled within appropriate social networks rather than left on low-income and often hostile estates. They should be entitled and required to take lessons in English language and culture, for which sufficient funding is essential. They should be officially welcomed as part of the process of naturalisation, in such a way as to emphasise their legitimacy within society and to make them (and the host nation) appreciative of the successful asylum application.

This much, whilst by no means uncontroversial, is less contentious than the painfully difficult question of having an asylum policy that not only welcomes and affirms the vulnerable but acts as a genuine deterrent to the disingenuous. David Blunkett's time at the Home Office has seen a raft of such restrictive legislation and earned him the reputation as a tough Home Secretary. It has, however, been largely successful in reducing the number of asylum applicants, which suggests, in lieu of a point made in chapter 2, that domestic policy does have an impact on asylum, in spite of the dominance of 'push' factors.

Some of these policies, such as making airlines on certain routes copy passengers' passports before they depart, introducing video surveillance at appropriate points of entry and making it a criminal offence to advertise or offer immigration advice without proper qualifications appear sensible and are quite consonant with the principles outlined above.

Others, such as the reduction of legal aid, restricting the number of appeals to just one and ensuring the fast-track deportation of those who have already claimed asylum in safe third countries, may leave us more hesitant. In spite of the commendable objective of streamlining the system and making fraudulent claims more difficult, we must ask whether the leading principle of showing mercy and humanity towards the vulnerable is being obscured in the search for efficiency. Will, for example, quite reasonable efforts to reduce the legal aid bill and tackle those exploiting the appeals system lead, albeit unintentionally, to the neglect or injudicious treatment of those with especially complex cases?

The answer to this question and the broader one of a policy's overall success will depend on the balance of two types of evidence: the 'hard' data of the policy's achievements and the 'soft' data of its impact on genuine claimants. The need for such a careful evaluation precludes the simplistic conclusion: 'this policy is/isn't Christian'. However, it is the author's opinion that policies that risk unfairness to individual applicants in the pursuit of a more efficient and more equitable system for the majority must be scrutinised carefully and required to prove their merits before being deemed acceptable.

Still other policies, such as the threat to take into care the children of failed applicants who refuse to return home, will leave us feeling distinctly nervous. Although this idea is not quite as black and white as it was sometimes reported – it is, after all, hardly caring to leave children to the destitution that results from their parents' failed claim and refusal to comply with the law – any policy which countenances parent-child separation, with all its dehumanising effects, cannot be acceptable in the long run.

These are just a handful of examples of policies that have been implemented or proposed as means of addressing the 'legality and justice' side of the debate. They are by their nature unpalatable, and Christians will rightly campaign to redress those they deem un-acceptable. Nonetheless, it is also important to extend sympathy to policy makers whose task it is to ensure legality and justice without infringing on mercy and humanity. All too often, the call to create the fast, efficient, fair and humane system that everyone wants requires not simply knowledge, nerve and foresight but also the wisdom of Solomon.

International asylum policy*

Domestic asylum issues are just one aspect of a much broader picture. As discussed above, asylum is a truly global phenomenon and it is, accordingly, easier to address it as such.

* This section draws in particular on *States of Conflict: Causes and patterns of forced migration to the EU and policy responses* by Stephen Castles, Heaven Crawley and Sean Loughna (London: IPPR, 2003)

In spite of all the controversies which rage in any single sovereign state, the wider picture encourages accord rather than discord. The one fact everyone agrees on is that the ideal number of refugees and asylum applicants is zero. Refugees and asylum applicants, by definition, are people who are running away from situations that should not exist in a just world.

Domestic asylum policy is so difficult because it is born of conflict, pain and tyranny and, ultimately, can only ever be a band aid. Genuine solutions to asylum must address its causes and not its effects, and this will involve a concerted international effort. This necessarily leads us into the area of the changing international order, a topic beyond the scope of this book, but worth briefly touching on in order to examine a few ideas that would have a positive impact on the causes of asylum.

Early warning systems and an effective mechanism for rapid reaction are important means of addressing refugee-producing conflicts before they begin or, more realistically, before they escalate. Unfortunately, this is a policy the success of which can never be known, as nobody can ever say what the alternative might have been. It is also an enormously controversial area, involving, for example, the development of international armies, such as the European Rapid Reaction Force, and the potential for pre-emptive military action, seven examples of which occurred in the 1990s alone – with varying levels of success.[5] That said, it need not entail the use of force, about which Christians will naturally be wary, as there is a wide range of preventative diplomatic measures, from mediation to sanctions, which are available. Problematic as it is, this approach still offers the potential of being the most effective single way of reducing global refugee and asylum figures in the future.

If prevention proves impossible, humanitarian intervention is vital. Such action is often, like asylum policy itself, a bandaid, and a self-interested one at that. More and more nations recognise that localised, refugee-creating conflicts have a habit of destabilising entire regions by creating economic disruption, mass people movements and recruiting grounds for terrorist organisations. Yet, humanitarian intervention is all the more likely to be effective for being self-interested.

Over the longer term, international pressure to improve and safeguard human rights in those nations from whom the majority of the world's refugees come is important, as is the targeted deployment of development aid. It is universally recognised that 'development policy can in the long run play a major role in conflict prevention, and hence in reducing forced migration', and as such is highly cost effective in the final reckoning, even if it reduces domestic budgets in the short term.[6]

Ultimately, it has been argued that the most important measures to reduce asylum applicant flows have no direct connection with migration at all but are rather to be found in trade and investment policy. 'It has long been argued by economists that the most effective way of encouraging development is through policies designed to bring about free trade and include less developed countries in global economic relationships' – a theory hardly reflected in the fact that, according to one recent estimate, 'trade restrictionism by rich countries costs low-income countries around $100 billion a year: twice as much as they receive in aid.'[7]

Some of these ideas are uncontroversial, whereas others, such as those that imply the overruling of national sovereignty, will set alarm bells ringing. Yet, however one views them, the one undeniable fact is that domestic asylum policy does not and cannot exist in a vacuum. Without the much-vaunted 'joined-up thinking' between domestic, foreign and economic policies, government budgets will be slowly wasted on problems which have causes and effects far wider than that of any one department's scope. In the words of one recent report, 'the current separate (and often conflicting) policies on poverty reduction, globalisation, security, refugees and migration are costly and counterproductive.'[8]

Immigration policy

The many layers of the immigration debate advise against attempting a detailed policy review, even if such a thing were possible. Instead, in the same way as the asylum policy analysis looked at the general contours of the debate, we will revisit the various layers of the immigration debate as discussed above and, equipped with biblical principles, attempt to offer a Christian perspective on each of these.

Demographics and economics As already noted, the demographic question is something of a red herring. Although much of the immigration debate is indeed about population size and balance, neither of these factors signify anything when taken in isolation. Instead, when the debate proceeds, as it must, to issues of economics, the demographic question becomes meaningful and biblical principles can offer substantive guidance.

The underlying biblical theme that money, whilst not being intrinsically evil, is not the measure of all things and should not be treated as the objective of any society, is a good place to start.[9] This principle stands in direct tension with opinions which claim (in as many words) that we need more people to maintain the economy. Such attitudes, usually and frequently voiced as a reason for immigration, are unacceptable as they effectively invert the Christian worldview. Money should be our slave, not our master. The economy should serve society, not the other way round. The argument that we need people in order to feed the economy treats people as a fuel and the economy as the machine that needs maintenance at any cost. This is not so much an argument against immigration, as against a purely economic justification for it. If immigration is a good idea, it should be for the good of people, not for the good of the cash register.

It will be argued, in response to this, that the good of the cash register ultimately *is* the good of the people but whereas that argument might have been justifiable 50 years ago, it skates on thin ice today. The last half century in the West has seen GDP per capita grow exponentially and yet, as far as it can be measured, levels of personal happiness have not only not followed it but have begun to decline. More money does not mean more joy.

From a Christian perspective, where societies today treat wealth as the key to and best measure of a nation's success or health, biblical teaching understands relationships as a far better tool and metric. The post-war economic boom, in spite of it many positive effects, has put relationships under enormous pressure, in such a way that it is hardly surprising that people are generally less happy with life today than they were in 1950. If a well-fed economy has failed to preserve our relationships or our happiness over the last half century, the *economic* argument for further large-scale immigration is ill-advised, to put it kindly.

As if further justification were needed, the Christian perspective also strongly advises against the argument that claims that the UK needs immigrants in order to do the lower paid jobs that UK-born people allegedly do not want to do themselves. Quite apart from the distasteful implications of this argument – that some or all of the million or so currently unemployed people do not want to work – it is one with potentially dreadful repercussions. Not only is it degrading to import foreigners to do the work that nationals are not prepared to do themselves but it almost inevitably creates and stores up socio-economic tension for the future. Not only are the wages of current lower paid employees potentially depressed, something that alienates the existing low-paid and naturally breeds resentment, but an underclass of low-paid, immigrant workers is created. When those immigrants are from ethnic minority groups, as they often are, the resultant situation is one where 'the colour line is the power line is the poverty line'.[10] What appears, at first, is economic sense soon becomes social segregation. If immigration is to be recommended for the UK, it needs to be on other than economic grounds.

Society and environment   The biblical vision of human well-being coming from relationships rather than just money, directs us away from economic arguments towards the third and fourth levels of the debate: society and environment, two areas that point us beyond the basic numbers question.

British society has moved a long way since the days when 'no Blacks, no Irish, no dogs' signs were put up in boarding houses, but few would claim it has moved far enough. Biblical teaching is insistent on the fundamental unity of mankind and of society's responsibility towards aliens irrespective of the level of their integration. As such, the continuing presence of racist elements within areas in British society, not least official bodies, is unacceptable. Whether it is in the police, the Crown Prosecution Service, the courts, employment practices, or in casual conversation, attitudes which deny people their humanity, dignity or their basic legal and economic rights simply because they are immigrants or children of immigrants cannot be tolerated.

The flip side to this essentially negative point is the need to establish a positive affirmation of immigration, not so much by demanding significantly more but by treating current immigration with official pride and recognition. It is often commented that citizenship ceremonies in many countries round the world are serious, solemn affairs in which immigrants are officially welcomed into a nation and community, after some combination of application, interview and examination. The almost complete absence of this in the UK leaves a painful grey area, where individuals are or are perceived to be less than completely part of society.

This point touches on two major current issues in particular: citizenship and ID cards. The absence of any established concept of British citizenship saw the Labour government set up an advisory board, headed by Sir Bernard Crick, to examine what citizenship entails and how it might be engrafted into British society. As already quoted, the group's objective was 'not ... to define Britishness [but] ... to define what people need to settle in effectively.'

Crick's report recommends 'a sufficient understanding of English, Welsh or Scottish Gaelic' and 'a sufficient understanding of UK society and civic structures.' Under its 'Living in the UK' programme, it calls for a basic knowledge of relevant sources of help and information, employment, everyday needs, the law, Britain as a changing multicultural society, and British national institutions. The group also examined the teaching of citizenship at school, recommending the teaching of 'the knowledge, skills and values relevant to the nature and practices of participative democracy', the 'duties, responsibilities, rights and development of pupils into citizens', and 'the value to individuals, schools and society of involvement in the local and wider community'. Complementing this, the Nationality, Immigration and Asylum White Paper required applicants for British citizenship to pass an English language test, recommended a citizenship ceremony involving an oath of allegiance, and gave power to take British nationality away if a British citizen has done anything 'seriously prejudicial to the vital interests of the UK'.

Alongside this, a plan to introduce identity cards within a decade was unveiled in the 2003 Queen's speech. This spoke about a centralised database and compulsory cards with personal biometric data, which would be used to tackle illegal working and immigration, to disrupt organised crime and terrorism, and to prevent abuse of public services and benefits. This draft bill is highly controversial, particularly over the issues of public service usage (under the bill ministers would have power to change the system to prevent people using specific public services if they do not produce a valid ID card) and compulsion (it is not clear whether the carrying or production of ID cards would become compulsory and what the penalties for non-production would be). Moreover, it is not entirely clear what its benefits would be: France runs a compulsory identity card system without significant loss of liberty but also without significant reduction in benefit fraud and organised crime. Furthermore, the introduction of ID cards will be expensive and hopes that the use of biometric data will make the cards somehow beyond the criminal fraternity's abilities are frankly naïve.

Nevertheless, in spite of all these practical problems, current explorations of citizenship and identity cards are to be welcomed as means of dispelling the fog that surrounds much immigration policy and treating the 'alien within your walls' in a more official and positive way. They are, in a modern, non-religious way, a faint imitation of a covenantal agreement, with its emphasis on mutual openness, loyalty, obligation and trust.

These various policies – the attack on prejudice, the positive and official affirmation of immigration through citizenship ceremonies and education, the classes on English language, culture and society for immigrants, and the exploration of the merits of citizenship and identity cards – are all aimed at encouraging integration and addressing the implicit segregation that exists in many of the social areas discussed above. They are all, practical reservations aside, consonant with biblical teaching on the position of 'alien' within society.

There are other, less momentous and tendentious ways, in which this integration might be encouraged. As research has shown, it is not immigration itself that is a criterion for successful economic and occupational integration but education, qualifications, English language fluency, knowledge of the UK labour market, relevant work experience, and the level of discrimination experienced. Providing English language teaching, offering careers advice and arranging with foreign governments for the easier translation of foreign qualifications to the UK labour market (such as already exist in medicine) could all take their place alongside more obvious anti-discrimination policy as a means of fostering integration in the workforce and thereby in the economy. From the host nation's point of view, a greater emphasis on understanding the immigrant experience would benefit many people and could constitute part of the national curriculum. Similarly, civic education courses at schools and universities would help foster a sense of welcome.

Biblical principles offer another important perspective on this issue, however, and it is one we ignore at our cost.

Anti-immigration sentiments and support for far-right parties may often have their roots in outright racism but they grow in the soil of low-income, native communities which feel as if they are being bypassed in favour of (as they see it) less deserving immigrants. Resentment is further fed when such economically vulnerable communities feel that it is the far more comfortable, suburban, middle-class policy makers who make the decisions on their behalf.

The continuous bracketing of the alien with the widow and the fatherless in biblical teaching is an important point in this context. It suggests, as outlined above, that one vulnerable group is not to be favoured over another, and that responsibility to deprived Israelites was not to be disregarded in favour of responsibility towards needy aliens. In a nation in which the gap between top and bottom income deciles has grown significantly over the last two decades and where the number of children living in low-income households remains over three million, this is no small consideration.

Initiatives to integrate immigrants and their children economically must have counterpart strategies for low-income UK families. Indeed, it is perhaps better to ignore the UK-born/immigrant division in this area of policy altogether, and focus instead on socio-economic strata within society. Many immigrants will require less financial help and encouragement from the government than many UK-born families, and policy must therefore be careful not to prioritise the education, training, advice and economic support of immigrants over that of low-income native families simply because they are immigrants.

When we turn from the social to the environmental element of the immigration debate, we maintain our focus on relationships but broaden it to explore how those relationships are rooted and contextualised in time and place. In doing so we also naturally return to the question of optimum immigration levels.

The biblical vision of society is one in which people are embodied and rooted in their environment.[11] Relationships do not exist in a vacuum. The true 'essence' of human beings is in their bodily reality and not in any abstract, Platonic soul or spirit. The social aspects of the immigration debate must, therefore, consider their environmental impact. How and where we live, work, shop, travel and relax has a vital impact on who we are.

Mankind's stewardship role, as outlined in the opening chapters of Genesis, is important in this context.[12] As leaseholders rather than freeholders of the land, the Israelites could and did have their tenancy rights revoked for failing to maintain their side of the agreement. In a similar way, mankind's brief tenancy of creation, with his attendant rights and responsibilities, is an underlying theme within biblical teaching. It is hardly surprising that aggressively human-centred, utopian projects, such as Soviet Russia's, result in environmental as well as social catastrophe. The earth, and everything in it, is the Lord's, not ours.

Precisely how this mandate is applied to current population issues and the attendant question of optimum immigration levels is a slippery issue. We may be instructed not to abuse the environment in pursuit of our own happiness, but whether a new housing development that encroaches on rural land constitutes an 'abuse' is questionable. Many people are concerned with the gradual erosion of the rural landscape that is not only the backbone of historic British identity but also one of the most attractive reasons for living in the UK. However deep this concern is, though, it is important not to hijack Genesis 1–3 to justify what is often an intensely personal feeling.

That said, there can be little doubt that the unlimited immigration, as outlined as a government policy by David Blunkett in 2003, would have catastrophic consequences on the environment. The environment is a zero-sum game and even if social infrastructure could cope with a population density greater than present – and evidence from the South-East suggests otherwise – few feel that the landscape *or the people living in it* would benefit from many millions more houses. One alternative of using brown field sites as development land is responsible and attractive but of limited potential. Another, of optimising urban population density by reducing the size of living units in the future, is unlikely to be popular.

Canny politicians may refuse to slap a figure on the optimum national population and immigration level but it is hard to believe that such a figure does not exist if we are to exercise any stewardship role over our particular corner of creation. By means of their research technique of 'ecological footprinting', the organisation Optimum Population Trust claim that, 'a population of 30 million may be the largest that the UK can sustain throughout the next century if its continuing damage to local and global environments is to stop and its citizens are to enjoy an acceptable quality of life.' It concludes that 'the most urgent short-term population policy needs to be a demographically balanced (net zero effect on population growth) migration policy.'[13]

Precise estimates and calculations will, of course, be controversial but it seems that environmental and social infrastructure considerations constitute the most persuasive reason not so much to limit immigration as to limit *net* immigration. Environmental concerns have nothing to say about the *makeup* of a population but are highly instructive concerning its size, and Britain's (not to mention England's) relatively high population density suggests that future, large-scale immigration could be seriously injurious. It should be emphasised, however, that this argument may only be deployed with care: using population density as a reason against immigration is less than wholly convincing when the immigrants in question come from Bangladesh.

Culture British culture would have undergone seismic changes in the second half of the twentieth century had there been no large-scale immigration. The presence of millions of individuals who were not born in the UK merely brought the question of who the British are into sharp focus.

Biblical guidance must be treated with extreme caution at this point. Israel is not a model to be imitated directly, its unique characteristics making modern national imitation singularly inappropriate. Instead, biblical teaching does have *general* principles that can guide our thinking here.[14] Just as, on an international scale, the Bible bears witness to 'the value of a plurality of nations and the universal validity of a single ethical code', on a national scale it suggests two principles of internal organisation: 'a principle of personal liberty and a principle of cultural integration.' This is close to the 'unity with diversity' that is so often talked about, or to put it another way, a common culture with liberty of conscience. However expressed, it has become something of a modern day Holy Grail, with little consensus on the right balance between personal liberty and cultural integration.

The biblical recognition of assimilating and non-assimilating *gerim* and its vision of graduated integration addressed this tension by suggesting that a) the culture of the host nation is a genuine entity, b) integration into it must be a matter of personal choice, c) refusal to integrate should not incur loss of legal or economic rights, but d) refusal to integrate should preclude full cultural rights, such as presence at the Passover.

Translating these principles is not easy. The first acts as a check on the impact of the kind of revisionist history that seeks to dismantle the traditional structure of British history in order to serve current cultural agendas. As George Orwell so rightly observed, who controls the past controls the present, and the recent battle over history teaching is anything but an arcane exercise in historiography or educational practice. At the same time, just as revisionism should not be used as a tool for cultural engineering, fidelity to a nation's history should not prevent ongoing reassessment of its past. Loyalty must ultimately be to the truth, although that is a slippery beast when it comes to the study of history. Historical re-evaluation needs to be treated with caution but must not be shied away from for fear of upsetting the national historical applecart.

The second point – that integration must be a matter of personal choice – is easy to swallow in a culture shaped by liberalism, as is the third, that refusal to integrate should not lose you your fundamental 'rights'. The fourth, however, is more challenging and demands a careful look at the modern equivalents of Israel's beliefs, vision, festivals, symbols, stories and praxes. To a limited degree this will emerge with the exploration of citizenship but culture is a rather more subtle beast and demands a more detailed study.

Studying culture is only the first step in the process, however, as the results must be applied to have any effect whatsoever. How this happens is again debatable, but might include an ongoing national cultural commission and national cultural exhibition, after the fashion of the

Great Exhibition, the Festival of Britain and (dare one even mention it?) the Millennium Dome. Cultural education should perhaps play a role in schools and universities, with a working knowledge of national history, society, politics and constitution being mandatory not just for immigrants but for all who profess and call themselves British. The allegiance to nation and flag which forms such an important part of the US identity is sneered at in some UK quarters but has much to recommend it; arguably, it has achieved much in harmonising a country that has a considerably higher proportion of immigrants and is considerably more diverse than the UK.

The difficulty comes in how to encourage integration. Whilst integration was not compulsory in Israel, the alternative would not have been appealing to many *gerim*. It is neither attractive nor justifiable to suggest that cultural integration should be a necessary criterion for entitlement to public services – apart from anything else it would be infringing on the basic human dignity which non-assimilating aliens were guaranteed in legal and financial matters. But it is also naïve to suggest that cultural integration will simply happen because it seems like a nice idea. Whether it is through voting rights, full citizenship or some other mechanism, cultural integration will need a catalyst.

The caveat to be voiced (again) at this point is that modern British culture is not the same as early Israel's and should not need to be preserved at all costs. Encouraging integration should not become a subtle way of allowing national culture to ossify and preventing anything new from ever developing. There is much in the current cultural climate that, as Yasmin Alibhai-Brown's interviewee indicated, needs changing.

Instead, this point is simply a way of making sure that the 'diversity' which comes so naturally to our post-modern, liberalised selves is balanced by a degree of unity and cohesion. Any country that wishes to operate an extended welfare state like Britain's needs a degree of social and cultural cohesion. The alternative is much-reduced welfare provision and, more frighteningly, a society that when under pressure, because unable to draw on a sense of shared, cohesive values, fragments and turns violent.[15]

International relations   Finally, there is a need to consider the international aspects of the debate and, in particular, the impact that immigration has on international relations. We have already observed how domestic asylum policy takes its place within a wider international context, and the same must be said of immigration in general.

The international context, and the overwhelming Christian call to see justice done round the world and not just in one's own land, mean that other nations' well-being must be taken into consideration. Accepting qualified professionals from low-income countries so that one's own welfare state is staffed and ignoring the debilitating impact this can have on foreign systems is unacceptable. The remittance argument rationalising this is a palliative, not a justification.

At the same time, declining qualified professionals from low-income countries whose need for them is greater than ours should not become a substitute for other forms of investment. A national policy which restricts migration levels for the purpose of optimising the well-being of native citizens may be acceptable in its own right but becomes immoral if it breeds an isolationism which ignores the plight of foreigners who have been denied right of entry.

Practice

It is important that Christians have cogent principles with which to navigate the asylum and immigration debate, and evaluate and recommend policies. The alternative is to leave one's faith at the door of any meaningful discussion of the issues and to become dangerously exposed to the volatile winds of pragmatism and public opinion.

However, principles and policies are far from the end of the matter that, as we have emphasised throughout this discussion, is about the lives, hopes and fears of individuals, each of whom is made in God's image. To leave the discussion at a theoretical level is to abnegate the responsibility that Jesus explicitly lays on his followers in his teaching in Matthew chapter 25 or Luke chapter 10. It is, perhaps, to side with the priest or the Levite, with their expertise and perhaps even good intentions, rather than with the Samaritan, with his practical action.

It is therefore fitting to conclude with some pointers towards practical help and involvement in this whole area. What follows is neither a directory of Christian work in this area nor a would-be best practice manual. The 'Further Engaging' section below gives fuller details of Christian organisations (or those with Christian links) that offer both. Instead, it is a brief survey of a handful of current initiatives that seek to implement some of the thinking discussed in this book in practical and relevant ways. Hopefully it will act as a guide and spur for those interested in taking practical steps in their own localities.

In 2001 CityLife church in Southampton initiated CLEAR: City Life Education and Action for Refugees.[16] CLEAR supports asylum applicants who are awaiting their decision by helping them integrate and improve their spoken and written English, their quality of life and their employability.

Among the various projects run by CLEAR is a bicycle recycling workshop, which collects second-hand bikes from around the city which the asylum applicants then renovate in a workshop. The project provides them with a free bicycle, practical work, a friendly environment and a chance to practise their English, and was given a particular boost when *The Southampton Advertiser* ran a front-page news article on the project that resulted in over 100 Southampton residents donating a second-hand bicycle. Other projects include English classes (to supplement those offered by Southampton City College), information, advice and practical support, a drop-in centre, a music workshop and a fishing class. Its website includes details of these projects, as well as refugee stories, facts and figures, and information about volunteering.

The whole project works in partnership with other organisations in the city which have formed The Southampton Refugee Umbrella Group – an information-sharing forum for the refugee voluntary sector in Southampton – and has developed a co-ordinated framework intended to prevent unnecessary project overlap.

Although initiated by CityLife church, the project relies on over 30 volunteers at any one time. These are people who are prepared to befriend and give practical assistance to asylum applicants, to help with informal English teaching workshops, to provide transport for medical appointments, to accompany individuals to formal interviews, or to fundraise for project costs. The whole initiative was made possible by sponsorship from numerous sources, including the Church Urban Fund, Southampton City Council and the Tudor Trust.

Praxis, based in East London and founded as a project of the Robert Kemble Christian Institute in 1983, is another example of a local organisation reaching out and helping asylum applicants in a particular locality.[17] With some foresight the project recognised that, in the wake of the Cold War, population displacement would become a key global issue, and so developed a practical programme to tackle problems of impoverishment and displacement within the local context of Inner London.

Today Praxis employs over twenty staff members and at its East London premises offers a hall for community events, rooms for advice and training, and facilities for music, art and drama. The organisation offers a walk-in advice service, counselling, work training, an accommodation scheme, and a volunteer programme for health and social care trainees. It assists emerging refugee community organisations outside London, operates a support service to enable probation, health and social care professionals to work better with refugee and asylum applicants, and facilitates initiatives from within the refugee community, providing cultural and social activities along with mutual support. Praxis's slogan 'A place for people displaced' is not simply well-suited to the organisation's work but also accurately reflects the plight of and scriptural call to help the 'alien' and 'stranger'.

On a slightly different level, the ECSR group – Enabling Christians in Serving Refugees – is an invaluable resource for Christians or churches who wish to engage practically in this area.[18] Its mission statement is 'Assisting and equipping Christians to express God's love in practical and informed ways to asylum seekers and refugees in the UK'. It does this by offering resources, support and encouragement to Christians who either are or wish to become involved with asylum, voluntarily or professionally, and by linking up asylum applicant and refugee support initiatives across the country. Its challenge to Christians is explicit: '[The] challenge for many Christians in the UK [is] to put Matthew 25:35 – "I was a stranger and you welcomed me" – into practice and welcome the "strangers" living in our communities.'

ECSR's website presents a long list of local, national and international organisations which deal with asylum, and then gives relevant and useful details concerning detention and reception, education, employment, health and project development. Unlike CLEAR or Praxis, ECSR does not institute or run projects itself, but for those eager to involve either themselves or their churches in such work, it offers a valuable resource.

Finally, the Churches' Commission for Racial Justice (CCRJ) has, as the name suggests, a broader remit than simply asylum and immigration.[19] These topics are naturally central to its work, however, which is overall concerned with co-ordinating the Churches' response (it works ecumenically) to key issues of racial justice. One of its remits is monitoring UK and European public policy on issues of asylum, immigration, race relations and economic and social issues, in which capacity it published *Asylum Voices*, a research document drawn on in this book. It also collaborates on campaigns to support the victims of racial abuse in the areas of asylum and immigration, administers the Bail Circle, which offers sureties, legal and financial support, and gives time to immigration and asylum detainees who have no contacts in the UK, and, as part of an ongoing task, provides theological reflection and a framework for all racial justice work. CCRJ clearly operates across a broader spectrum than the three previous examples but it remains a key resource of help and guidance for Christians interested in asylum and immigration.

These four examples, each operating at a different level with different objectives, offer a brief indication of some of the initiatives currently running in the UK that put aspects of the thinking discussed above into practice. More details are given in the 'Further Engaging' section below.

Such specific projects are an integral part of the Christian response to the issues of asylum and immigration in Britain today. They are not, however, a substitute for clear, up-to-date and biblically rooted thinking, which can help navigate us through the minefield of confused definitions and slippery statistics, and understand and evaluate the issues in their entirety.

Isolated from one another, social action becomes a band aid and critical thinking becomes toothless theorising. United, however, in a way that the UK Christian network with its four million plus active members could uniquely achieve, they are a powerful combination indeed.

Faith calls for just such a holistic response. As aliens and strangers in the world, God's call to us to love the alien as ourselves is challenging, sometimes difficult to work out and ultimately uncompromising. There are, however, fewer higher calls to which we can respond.

Further Reading

Books

Alibhai-Brown, Yasmin. *Who do we think we are?* (London: Penguin, 2000)

Browne, Anthony. *Do we need mass immigration?* (London: Civitas, 2002)

Burnside, Jonathan. *The Status and Welfare of Immigrants* (Cambridge: Jubilee Centre, 2001)

Hays, J. Daniel. *From every People and Nation: A biblical theology of race* (Illinois: IVP, 2003)

Koyzis, David. *Political Visions and Illusions* (Illinois: IVP, 2003)

Sacks, Jonathan. *The Dignity of Difference* (London: Continuum, 2002)

Temple, William. *Christianity and the Social Order* (London: Shepheard Walwyn, 1976)

Booklets

Alibhai-Brown, Yasmin. *True Colours: Public Attitudes to Multiculturalism and the Role of Government* (London: Institute for Public Policy Research, 1999)

Bradstock, Andrew, and Arlington Trotman, eds. *Asylum Voices* (London: Church House Publishing, 2003)

Castles, Stephen, Heaven Crawley and Sean Loughna. *States of Conflict: Causes and patterns of forced migration to the EU and policy responses* (London: IPPR, 2003)

Cooper, Robert. *The postmodern state and the world order* (London: Demos, 1996)

Johnston, O.R. *Nationhood: Towards a Christian Perspective* (Oxford: Latimer House, 1980)

Leonard, Mark. *Britain: Renewing our Identity* (London: Demos, 1997)

Logsdon, B.G.B. *Multipolarity and Covenant: Towards a Biblical Framework for Constitutional Safeguards* (Cambridge: Jubilee Centre, 1989)

Spencer, Nick. *Where do we go from here?: A biblical perspective on roots and mobility in Britain today* (Cambridge: Jubilee Centre, 2002)

Spencer, Nick. *The measure of all things: a biblical perspective on money and value in Britain today* (Cambridge: Jubilee Centre, 2003)

Cambridge papers

Rivers, Julian. *Multiculturalism* (Cambridge Papers, Vol. 10, No. 4, December 2001)

Rivers, Julian. *The New World Order?* (Cambridge Papers, Vol. 8, No. 4, December 1999)

Schluter, Michael. *Relationism: Pursuing a Biblical Vision for Society* (Cambridge Papers, Vol. 6, No. 4, December 1997)

Schluter, Michael. *Roots: Biblical Norm or Cultural Anachronism* (Cambridge Papers, Vol. 4 No. 4, December 1995)

Websites

Commission for Racial Equality: www.cre.gov.uk

COMPAS (Centre on Migration, Policy and Society): www.compas.ox.ac.uk

Home Office: www.homeoffice.gov.uk

Institute for Public Policy Research: www.ippr.org.uk

International Catholic Migration Commission: www.icmc.net

MigrationwatchUK: <u>www.migrationwatch.org</u>
Optimum Population Trust: <u>www.optimumpopulation.org</u>
Refugee Council: <u>www.refugeecouncil.org.uk</u>
UNHCR: <u>www.unhcr.ch</u>

Further Engaging

The Jubilee Centre: www.jubilee-centre.org

Seeks to offer a biblical vision for public life. Goal is to inspire and equip Christians to shape social and political life according to biblical principles. Provides research into and promotion of the biblical vision for society and its contemporary relevance.

CLEAR (City Life Education and Action for Refugees): www.clearproject.co.uk

Set up by City Life church in Southampton. Seeks to understand and respond to needs of asylum applicants in Southampton by support, personal advocacy, English teaching, transport, practical repair work and other projects.

ECSR (Enabling Christians in Serving Refugees): www.ecsr.org.uk

Website provides an extensive series of links to useful organisations and resources that offer information, resources and advice for assisting asylum seekers and refugees as they are integrated into life in the UK.

Tearfund: www.tearfund.org

Starting life as the Evangelical Alliance Refugee Fund in the 1960s, Tearfund works within the UK and internationally with asylum seekers, refugees and other poor communities, engaging in issues from poor accommodation to child exploitation.

CCRJ (Churches' Commission for Racial Justice): www.ctbi.org.uk/ ccrj

Ecumenical body concerned with issues of racial justice in the UK, with a particular interest in UK and European policy on asylum and immigration, and its consequences.

Further Study

Biblical teaching on asylum and immigration is extensive but scattered across both Old and New Testaments. Much of this teaching has been drawn on in chapters 4–7 of this book.

To encourage readers to take a closer look at the biblical material used in this book and to develop their own opinions on its message, a series of Bible studies is available on the Jubilee Centre website.

These explore passages from both Old and New Testament, placing them in their context and asking a number of questions about their meaning and relevance for today. They are written for house, cell or church groups, and can last anything from 30 minutes to over an hour each.

They are free and available at: www.jubilee-centre.org

About the Jubilee Centre

The Jubilee Centre was founded by Michael Schluter in 1983 from a conviction that the biblical social vision is relevant to the contemporary world, providing a coherent alternative to modern political ideologies.

This vision initially led the Jubilee Centre into a number of campaigning roles, in partnership with others, on such issues as Sunday trading (Keep Sunday Special) and credit & debt (Credit Action). It also led to the launch of The Relationships Foundation in 1994 to engage in practical initiatives to reform society, based a relational agenda or Relationism, on issues such as criminal justice, health, unemployment, business practice and peace building.

Over recent years the Jubilee Centre's focus has shifted away from campaigning towards promoting a coherent social vision based on careful research that applies biblical teaching to social, political and economic issues. It aims to share its work widely in order to equip Christians in the UK and overseas to shape society according to biblical principles.

The Jubilee Centre publishes its research regularly. Updates called *Engage* and *Cambridge Papers* are distributed free of charge each quarter. For further information about the Jubilee Centre, to order or access other publications (most are available free of charge, including past *Cambridge Papers*) or to join our free mailing list, please visit: www.jubilee-centre.org or contact us at:

Jubilee House
3 Hooper Street
Cambridge
CB1 2NZ
t: 01223 566319
e: info@jubilee-centre.org

Notes

Foreword

1. Section 55 prevents the Secretary of State from providing or arranging provision of support as required by the 1999 Act, if he is not satisfied that the person's asylum claim was made as soon as practicably possible after arrival in the UK.
2. Greater London Authority, *Destitute by Design* (February 2004).
3. Exodus 23:9

Chapter 1

1. Seamus Heaney, 'Whatever you say, say nothing', *North* (London: Faber & Faber, 1975)
2. cf. Yasmin Alibhai-Brown, *True Colours: Public Attitudes to Multiculturalism and the Role of Government* (London: Institute for Public Policy Research, 1999), pp.47–90
3. The phrase is, in fact, absent from the report itself but was used at the press conference, at least according to *The Guardian*. cf. 'Britain's schools dubbed racist', *The Guardian*, 11 March 1999 (http://www.guardian.co.uk/uk_news/story/0,3604,315727,00.html). For the OFSTED report itself

see http://www.ofsted.gov.uk/publications/docs/771.pdf.

4. 'Most Britons are racist, says prosecutions chief', *The Guardian*, 24 June 2002 (http://www.guardian.co.uk/uk_news/story/0,3604,742611,00.html)

5. Home Office Research Development Statistics, Immigration: http://www.homeoffice.gov.uk/rds/immigration1.html

6. Stephen Castles, Heaven Crawley and Sean Loughna, *States of Conflict: Causes and patterns of forced migration to the EU and policy responses* (London: IPPR, 2003)

7. Janet Dobson et al, *International migration and the United Kingdom: Recent patterns and trends* (Home Office RDS Occasional Paper No. 75) http://www.homeoffice.gov.uk/rds/pdfs/occ75execsum.pdf

8. Leslie Brown (ed.), *The New Shorter Oxford English Dictionary* (Oxford: Clarendon Press, 1933 (revised 1993)), p.1,315

9. *Migrants in the UK: their characteristics and labour market outcomes and impacts* (Home Office RDS Occasional Paper No. 82, 2002) p.4 (http://www.homeoffice.gov.uk/rds/pdfs2/occ82migrantuk.pdf)

10. The IPS interviews around 1 in 500 passengers, sampled on all major routes in and out of the UK. It questions them about their country of residence (for overseas residents) or country of visit (for UK residents), the reason for their visit, and details of their expenditure and fares. It defines as immigrants all those entering with work permits, or intending to work, for 12 months or more, students on long courses, spouses, fiancés, children and other dependants, although not asylum applicants. It addresses additional questions to this disparate group. For more details cf. http://www.statistics.gov.uk/ssd/surveys/international_passenger_survey.asp

11. Stephen Glover *et al*, *Migration: an economic and social analysis* (Home Office RDS Occasional Paper No. 67, 2001), p.10 (http://www.homeoffice.gov.uk/rds/pdfs/occ67-migration.pdf)

12. Christian Dustman *et al*, *Labour market performance of immigrants in the UK Labour market* (Home Office Online Report 05/03), p.70 http://www.homeoffice.gov.uk/rds/pdfs2/rdsolr0503.pdf

13. Article 1A(2) of 1951 Convention relating to the Status of Refugees (http://www.unhchr.ch/html/menu3/b/o_c_ref.htm)
14. IPPR, *States*, p.5
15. http://www.unhcr.ch/cgi-bin/texis/vtx/home/opendoc.htm?tbl=STATISTICS&id=3d075d374&page=statistics
16. Vaughan Robinson and Jeremy Segrott, *Understanding the decision-making of asylum seekers* (Home Office Research Study 243, 2002), p.vi. http://www.homeoffice.gov.uk/rds/pdfs2/hors243.pdf cf. also for further clarification and definitions (e.g. 'anticipatory asylum seeker', 'spontaneous asylum seeker', 'convention refugee')
17. IPPR, *States*, p.7
18. For example, Commission for Racial Equality, http://www.cre.gov.uk/gdpract/refuge.html#luxury; MigrationatchUK, http://www.migrationwatch.org/pdfs/Bulletin no2.pdf; Refugee Council, http://www.refugeecouncil.org.uk/news/myths/myth001.htm; BBC, http://news.bbc.co.uk/1/hi/uk/2173792.stm; Oxfam, http://www.oxfam.org.uk/policy/papers/asylumscot01/asylum.htm; *The Independent*, 23 May 2003, http://news.independent.co.uk/uk/politics/story.jsp?story=408727
19. http://www.mori.com/polls/2002/refugee.shtml. The correct answer to this question is itself very difficult to calculate. The global refugee population is a 'stock' figure, i.e. it gives the current stock of refugees. Conversely, national refugee populations are often not measured and national asylum ones are 'flow' figures, i.e. they measure the year-on-year flow of asylum applications rather than the stock of refugees. Whatever the correct figure is, it is certainly less than 23 per cent. See UNHCR statistics http://www.unhcr.ch/cgi-bin/texis/vtx/home?page=statistics for further details (NB their caveat in 2002 UNHCR Population Statistics, Table 2: 'In the absence of reliable Government figures, UNHCR has estimated the refugee population based on refugee arrivals and asylum-seeker recognition over the past 10 years for the following countries: Austria, Denmark, Finland, Iceland, Ireland, Italy, Netherlands, Norway, Portugal, Spain and UK.')
20. http://www.mori.com/polls/2003/migration.shtml

21. Robinson, *Decision-making*, p.viii
22. http://www.mori.com/digest/2000/pd001027.shtml. For further details on benefits available to asylum seekers, cf. http://www.statistics.gov.uk/downloads/theme_compendia/UK2003/UK2003.pdf p.91
23. http://www.mori.com/polls/2003/asylumseekers.shtml
24. And it is questionable whether the Norman Conquest or before it the Viking and Saxon invasions were numerically significant. See, for example, 'Teeth unravel Anglo-Saxon legacy', http://news.bbc.co.uk/1/hi/sci/tech/3514756.stm
25. *The Health Service Journal*, 12 November 1998, p.32; quoted in Harriet Sergeant, *No System to Abuse* (London: Centre for Policy Studies, 2003)
26. cf. IPPR, *States*, p.6; cf. also http://www.unhcr.ch/cgi-bin/texis/vtx/home?page=statistics
27. For example, 'There is a real need for more research in this area – indeed, it is striking how little research on migration there has been in the UK', in Glover et al, *Migration*, p.2
28. IPPR, *States*, p.2

Chapter 2

1. According to MORI's monthly State of the Nation polls: http://www.mori.com/polls/trends/issues.shtml
2. Home Office Asylum Statistics: 1st & 4th Quarter 2003. The number of applications is very different to the number of acceptances, which stood at 64,605 in 2003, reflecting the higher level of applications in 2001 and 2002.
3. 'Playing this crude numbers games plays into the hands of xenophobes', *The Independent*, 23 May 2003 http://news.independent.co.uk/uk/politics/story.jsp?story=408725
4. Home Office Asylum Statistics: 4th Quarter 2002 (http://www.homeoffice.gov.uk/rds/pdfs2/asylumq402.pdf)
5. Home Office Asylum Statistics: 1st Quarter 2002 (http://www.homeoffice.gov.uk/rds/pdfs/asylumq401.pdf)
6. Home Office Revisions to monthly asylum statistics for 2000 (http://www.homeoffice.gov.uk/rds/pdfs/asylumrev2k.pdf)

7. United Nations High Commissioner for Refugees (UNHCR), Asylum Applications in industrialised countries: 1980–1999 (Geneva, 2001) For this and other UNHCR statistics see http://www.unhcr.ch/cgi-bin/texis/vtx/statistics

8. http://www.unhcr.ch/static/statistics_2002/asr02-dr2-Table1.pdf

9. IPPR, *States*, p.6

10. UNHCR, *Asylum Levels and Trends: Europe and non-European Industrialized Countries, 2003*; http://www.unhcr.ch/cgi-bin/texis/vtx/home opendoc.pdf?tbl=STATISTICS&id=403b1d7e4&page=statistics

11. IPPR, *States, op. cit.*, p.17

12. Robinson, *Decision-making, op. cit.*

13. Home Office Asylum Statistics: 4th Quarter 2002 (http://www.homeoffice.gov.uk/rds/pdfs2/asylumq402.pdf)

14. Home Office Asylum Statistics: 4th Quarter 2001 (http://www.homeoffice.gov.uk/rds/pdfs/asylumq401.pdf)

15. Andrew Bradstock and Arlington Trotman (eds), *Asylum Voices* (London: Church House Publishing, 2003)

16. Robinson, *Decision-making*, p.vii

17. *Asylum Applications in Industrialised Countries* (Geneva: UNHCR, 2001) pp.144, 153–4

18. IPPR, *States*, p.29

19. cf. Harriet Sergeant, *No system to abuse: Immigration and Healthcare in the UK* (London: Centre for Policy Studies)

20. Robinson, *Decision-making*, p.1

21. cf. UNHCR statistics (http://www.unhcr.ch/cgi-bin/texis/vtx/statistics)

22. 'A Return to Powellism', *The Guardian*, 24 July 2003

23. Home Office Asylum Statistics: 4th Quarter 2003 (http://www.homeoffice.gov.uk/rds/pdfs/asylumq403.pdf)

24. cf. Mark Johnson, *Asylum seekers in dispersal – Healthcare issues* (Home Office, 2003: http://www.homeoffice.gov.uk/rds/pdfs2/rdsolr1303.pdf)

25. Andrea Eagle et al, *Asylum seekers' experiences of the voucher scheme in the UK – fieldwork report* (Home Office, March 2002: http://www.homeoffice.gov.uk/rds/pdfs2/asylumexp.pdf)

26. Churches' Commission for Racial Justice, *Safety and Security with Justice and Compassion: A Response to the UK Government's White Paper on Citizenship, Immigration and Asylum*

27. http://www.refugeecouncil.org.uk/downloads/briefings/nia_act_02/ed1_asylum.pdf
28. cf. *Asylum Voices*, pp.28–29 for a blackly comic example of misinterpretation during an interview
29. cf. *Asylum Voices*, pp.26–27
30. Particular concern has been expressed concerning the ongoing persecution of Roma in certain 'safe' countries.
31. For more questions and concerns see, for example, CCRJ, *Safety and Security, op. cit.*, Refugee Council. http://www.refugeecouncil.org.uk/downloads/briefings/nia_act_02/ed1_asylum.pdf; MigrationwatchUK, http://www.migrationwatchuk.org/pdfs/Response Asylum Applications.pdf; Shelter, http://www.shelter.org.uk/images/pdfs/campaign/asylumwhitepaper.pdf
32. See, for example, *Asylum Voice*, pp.22–47, http://www.guardian.co.uk/g2/story/0,3604,1046919,00.html
33. http://www.portal.telegraph.co.uk/news/main.jhtml?xml=%2Fnews%2F2003%2F06%2F15%2Fnhiv15.xml
34. David Walker, *The Numbers Game*, Analysis, BBC Radio 4, first broadcast 24 July 2003
35. David Blunkett, Response to asylum application figures Q1 2003, 22 May 2003, http://www.homeoffice.gov.uk/

Chapter 3

1. Stephen Byers, 'Asylum and Immigration', http://www.smf.co.uk/030730 byers.pdf, p.6
2. cf. *True Colours, op. cit.*, pp. 47–75; Anthony Browne, *Do we need mass immigration?* (London: Civitas, 2002), pp. 20–36, Glover et al, *op. cit.*, pp.19–26
3. Glover et al, *op. cit.*, p.7
4. Dobson et al, *op. cit.*, pp.11–12
5. Dobson et al, *op. cit.*, p.17
6. Dobson et al, *op. cit.*, p.39
7. Dobson et al, *op. cit.*, p.3
8. http://www.migrationwatch.org/pdfs/Projecting_immigration.pdf
9. Glover et al, *op. cit.*, p. 24

10. cf. http://www.gad.gov.uk/Publications/docs/
    population_trends_111.pdf, http://
    www.migrationwatch.org/BulletinNo7.asp
11. cf. Browne, *op. cit.*, p.21
12. Population Trends No. 112, (Summer 2003), http://
    www.statistics.gov.uk/downloads/theme_population/
    PT112.pdf, Table 2.1. 2002 figures are provisional.
13. Population Trends No. 112, Table 2.2. Total fertility rate is
    the number of children that would be born to a woman if
    current patterns of fertility persisted throughout her
    childbearing life. It is sometimes called the TPFR (total period
    fertility rate).
14. It should be noted that this is not known for certain, as TFR
    data are not available by immigrant breakdown. However,
    TFR is higher for those mothers born outside the UK than
    those born in it (2.2 vs. 1.6 in 2001), which acts as a good
    proxy. cf. Office for National Statistics, Series FM1 no. 31,
    Birth Statistics, Table 9.5 (http://www.statistics.gov.uk/
    downloads/theme_population/Fm1_31/FM1_31.pdf)
15. http://www.gad.gov.uk/news/
    national_population_projections_1998-based.htm
16. http://www.gad.gov.uk/Population/2001/methodology/
    assumptions.htm
17. The most recent forecasts, at the time of writing, from
    Population Trends 115 (Spring 2004), revised the projected
    2031 UK population to 64.8 million and offered the longer-
    term projection that the population would peak around 2050
    at over 65 million and then gradually start to fall.
18. In an article in Population Trends No. 109 (Autumn 2002),
    Chris Shaw of the GAD, forecast that under this 'LP' scenario
    the UK population would fall to around 55 million by 2050.
    He concluded that, 'There is considerable uncertainty about
    the future population size... [but] there is no inevitability
    about future population decline.' cf. http://
    www.statistics.gov.uk/downloads/theme_population/
    PT109.pdf
19. http://www.statistics.gov.uk/downloads/
    theme_population/PT115.pdf
20. http://www.statistics.gov.uk/downloads/
    theme_population/PT115.pdf. Longer-term projections
    show further ageing, with the median age eventually
    stabilising around 45 in the 2040s.

21. From 11.8 million in 2002 to 11 million in 2014. http://www.statistics.gov.uk/downloads/theme_population/PT115.pdf
22. From 10.9 million in 2002 to 12.7 million in 2021 to around 15 million in 2031. http://www.statistics.gov.uk/downloads/theme_population/PT115.pdf
23. http://www.gad.gov.uk/news/national_population_projections_1998-based.htm. Population Trends No. 115 (Spring 2004) modified these figures slightly: dependency ratio in 2002 was 620 dependants per 1,000 persons of working age. This would fall to about 600 in 2020 and then rise to 700 in the 2030s.
24. Glover et al, *op. cit.*, *Migration*, pp.4–5
25. Ceri Gott & Karl Johnston, *The migrant population in the UK: fiscal effects* (Home Office RDS Occasional Paper No. 77, 2002), p. iii; http://www.homeoffice.gov.uk/rds/pdfs/occ77migrant.pdf. An important footnote to this calculation reads, 'This is subject to a wide margin of error given that more accurate data is unavailable.'
26. Gott et al, *op. cit.*, p.11
27. Gott et al, *op. cit.*, figures 1 & 2
28. Gott et al, *op. cit.*, figure 4
29. Gott et al, *op. cit.*, figures 2 & 3
30. Gott et al, *op. cit.*, p.9
31. The higher level of self-employment 'perhaps support[s] anecdotal evidence that [immigrants] are more entrepreneurial than the UK-born population... [and] may also be a response to labour market barriers and may reflect disadvantage faced in gaining employment.' Gott et al, *op. cit.*, p.9
32. Jeremy Kempton (ed.), *Migrants in the UK: their characteristics and labour market outcomes and impacts* (Home Office RDS Occasional Paper No. 82, December 2002), p.5; http://www.homeoffice.gov.uk/rds/pdfs2/occ82migrantuk.pdf
33. UN Population Division, *Replacement Migration: Is it a solution to Declining and Ageing Populations?*: http://www.un.org/esa/population/publications/migration/migration.htm
34. Population Trends No. 103. p.45
35. Dobson et al, *International migration*, p.1
36. UN, *Replacement Migration, op. cit.*
37. Browne, *op. cit.*, pp.43–44

38. Richard Berthoud, *Poverty and prosperity among Britain's ethnic minorities* (Institute for Social and Economic Research, February 2002) p.3

39. Pierre Cuneo, *Ethnic Minorities' Economic Performance* (Performance and Innovation Unit, April 2001) p.13

40. Berthoud, *op. cit.*, p.3

41. The obvious attendant problem – that this method inevitably loses sight of white migrants beyond the first generation – is a regrettable result of the limited data.

42. Research has shown that language fluency increases the mean hourly occupational wage for ethnic minority migrant men by around 17 per cent.

43. Quoted in Browne, *op. cit.*, chapter 18

44. See, for example, Aslan Zorlu & Joop Hartog, *The effect of migration on native earnings* (University of Amsterdam, http:/ /www.lse.ac.uk/collections/EPIC/documents/ ICZorlu.pdf).

45. Kempton, *op. cit.*, p. 7. Note the discussion of wages remains at the population level and not with the unskilled workers that Layard discusses. See also, Gover, *op. cit.*; Christian Dustmann et al, *The local labour market effects of immigration in the UK* (Home Office Online Report 06/03: http:// www.homeoffice.gov.uk/rds/pdfs2/rdsolr0603.pdf)

46. Office for National Statistics, *UK 2003: The Official Yearbook of the United Kingdom and Northern Ireland* (Stationery Office, 2003), p.124. See also TUC report, *Moving on . . . How Britain's unions are tackling racism* (2004)

47. Glover, *op. cit.*, pp.38–9

48. Glover, *op. cit.*, p.39

49. Cuneo, *op. cit.*, pp.2–4

50. Glover, *op. cit.*, pp.39–42

51. cf. John Solomos, *Democratic Governance and Ethnic Minority Political Participation in Contemporary Britain* (ESRC, 2003)

52. The Electoral Commission, *Voter engagement among black and minority ethnic communities*, 2002 (http:// www.electoralcommission.org.uk/files/dms/ ethnic_voting_6600-6190__E__N__S__W__.pdf)

53. Solomos, *op. cit.*, p. 14

54. Commission for Racial Equality, *Factsheet: Ethnic Minorities in Britain*. NB this data comes from the 1991 census and is therefore rather out of date. More recent data do not appear to be available.

55. See, for example, Richard Layard, 'Happiness: Has Social Science a Clue', The Lionel Robbins Memorial Lectures, 2002/3; Roger Levett, *A Better Choice of Choice* (London: Fabian Society, 2003); www.oswald.ac.uk

56. Levett, *op. cit.*, p.1. Emphases mine.

57. Office for National Statistics, *UK 2003: The Official Yearbook of the United Kingdom of Great Britain and Northern Ireland* (The Stationery Office, 2003), p.292; http://www.statistics.gov.uk/downloads/theme_compendia/UK2003/UK2003.pdf

58. http://www.cpre.org.uk/campaigns/planning/communities-not-concrete/what-is-the-problem.htm

59. For starters see Yasmin Alibhai-Brown, *Who do we think we are?* (Penguin, 2000); *True Colours, op. cit., The Parekh Report, op. cit;* Richard Weight, *Patriots* (London: Macmillan, 2002); Mark Leonard, *Britain: Renewing our Identity* (Demos, 1997). For a Christian viewpoint see Julian Rivers, *Multiculturalism* (Cambridge Papers, Volume 10, Number 4, December 2001)

60. T.S. Eliot, *Notes towards the definition of culture* (Faber & Faber, 1948), p.31

61. Banned under British and Indian law, but still practised occasionally in India.

62. Banned under British law but still practised clandestinely in Britain.

63. Banned under British law but a subject of much debate.

64. Permitted under British law but called to be banned in a report from the Farming and Animal Welfare Council in 2003.

65. Permitted under British law but a subject of much controversy in Germany and France. It is a fascinating example of the central paradox of the culturally omni-tolerant position, in which committed liberals refuse to tolerate headscarves because they see them as signs of an intolerant religion. http://news.bbc.co.uk/1/hi/world/europe/3135600.stm

66. Browne, *op. cit.*, pp.129–134. A report published by the Inter-American Development Bank in April 2004 claimed that remittance payments were now the largest source of investment in Latin America. In 2003, Hispanic workers living in industrialised countries sent home $38bn.

67. *The Accra Mail*, 12 August 2002, quoted in Browne, *op. cit*.

68. cf. Organisation for Social Science Research in Eastern and Southern Africa

69. James Buchan et al., *International Nurse Mobility: Trends and Policy Implications* (http://www.rcn.org.uk/downloads/ InternationalNurseMobility-April162003.doc); see also Steve Fouch, 'Globalisation and health' (Christian Medical Fellowship files, No. 24)

Chapter 4

1. Psalm 119.14–16
2. Matthew 5.17–19
3. 2 Timothy 3.16
4. Deuteronomy 4.40
5. Jonathan Burnside, *The Status and Welfare of Immigrants* (Cambridge: Jubilee Centre, 2001), pp. 2–3
6. J. Daniel Hays, *From every People and Nation: A biblical theology of race* (Illinois: IVP, 2003), pp.25–45, 141–56
7. Genesis 12.1–3
8. Genesis 24, 28.1–5
9. Genesis 38
10. Genesis 46.10
11. Genesis 41
12. Genesis 41.50
13. Hays, *op. cit.*, p.33
14. Exodus 12.38
15. Hays, *op. cit.*, p.65–68, Burnside, *op. cit.*, p.1–2
16. Walter Brueggemann, 'The Book of Exodus', in L. E. Keck (ed.), *The New Interpreter's Bible*, Vol. 1 (Nashville: Abingdon, 1994), p.781
17. Exodus 12.43–49
18. Burnside, *op. cit.*, p.2
19. 2 Chronicles 2.17–18, 1 Chronicles 22.2
20. Genesis 23.3–4
21. Hebrews 11.8–10, 13–16
22. Exodus 1.8–10. The modern echoes of this, such as in France's concern that permitting the wearing of headscarves among the growing Muslim population will act as a green light to anti-French religious extremism, are sometimes uncanny.
23. Exodus 1.12

24. Jonathan Sacks, *The Dignity of Difference* (London: Continuum, 2002), p.59
25. Exodus 23.9, Leviticus 19.34, Deuteronomy 26.5, 1 Chronicles 29.15, etc.
26. Leviticus 25.23
27. Sacks, *op. cit.*, p.58
28. 1 Peter 1.1, 1.17, 2.11
29. 'The First Epistle of Clement to the Corinthians', in Louth. A (ed.) *Early Christian Writings: The Apostolic Fathers* (London: Penguin Books, 1968 (rev. 1987), p.23
30. 'Letter to Diognetus', in ibid., pp.144–145
31. Burnside, *op. cit.*, p.6
32. Leviticus 25.47–50
33. See Sacks, *op. cit.*, chapter 3 for a very interesting discussion on this point.
34. Genesis 17.5, 18.18, 22.18, 26.4
35. Deuteronomy 4.5–6
36. Isaiah 2.2, 11.10, 52.10, 56.7; cf. Hays, *op. cit.*, pp.106–116
37. Revelation 5.9, 7.9, cf. Hays, *op. cit.*, pp.193–99

Chapter 5

1. Christiana Van Houten, *The Alien in Biblical Law* (Sheffield: Sheffield Academic Press, 1991), p.139; quoted in Burnside, *op. cit.*, p.10
2. Burnside, *op. cit.*, pp.17–20
3. e.g. Isaiah 2.5–8, Psalm 144.7–8, Isaiah 62.8, Hosea 7.8–13
4. 1 Kings 8.41–43
5. cf. Burnside, *op. cit*, pp.10–16
6. Exodus 20.10
7. e.g. Leviticus 19.34, 25.35, Deuteronomy 10.19
8. Burnside, *op. cit.*, p.15
9. Exodus 12.49
10. Deuteronomy 24.17, 27.19
11. Exodus 20.9–11, 22.21, 23.9
12. Leviticus 19.9–10, 23.22, Deuteronomy 24.19–22
13. Deuteronomy 24.14–15
14. Deuteronomy 14.28–29, 26.12–13
15. Numbers 35.15

16. Ezekiel 47.21–23
17. Exodus 12.43–49
18. Leviticus 16.29
19. Deuteronomy 29.10–13, 31.12
20. Leviticus 17.8–9, 22.18, Numbers 15.14
21. Exodus 12.19
22. Numbers 15.29
23. Numbers 15.30
24. Leviticus 24.10–16
25. Leviticus 24.17–22
26. Leviticus 18.26
27. http://www.bisnis.doc.gov/BISNIS/BULLETIN/apr02bull4.htm
28. Ezekiel 47.21–23
29. Deuteronomy 15.2–3
30. Deuteronomy 23.20
31. Exodus 12.43
32. Deuteronomy 17.15
33. Deuteronomy 23.1–8, Ezekiel 44.6–9
34. cf. Deuteronomy 12.29–31, 20.16–18, 7.3–4, Ezra 9–10
35. Deuteronomy 23.3–6, Nehemiah 13.1–3
36. Deuteronomy 20.10–15
37. Deuteronomy 23.7–8
38. Deuteronomy 9.4–6
39. Burnside, *op. cit.*, p.49
40. Amos 9.7
41. Micah 6.8
42. Ezekiel 22.6–7
43. Ezekiel 22.29
44. Jeremiah 7.4–7
45. Jeremiah 22.3–5
46. Zechariah 7.10
47. Malachi 3.5
48. Matthew 5.17–19
49. Leviticus 19.34, Deuteronomy 10.18–19
50. Luke 10.25–37
51. Josephus, *Antiquities* 18.29–30, cf. Hays, *op. cit.*, p.166
52. Josephus, *Antiquities* 20.118–136, cf. Hays, *op. cit.*, p.166
53. Luke 17.11–19
54. Luke 9.51–56
55. Acts 1.8

56. Acts 8.4–25, 15.3–4
57. Hays, *op. cit.*, p.159
58. C.S. Kenner, *A Commentary on the Gospel of Matthew* (Grand
    Rapids, Eerdmans, 1999), p.80, Hays, *op. cit.*, p.159
59. Matthew 25.34–40

Chapter 6

1. Robert Cooper, *The postmodern state and the world order*
   (London: Demos, 1996), pp.4–5
2. Cooper, *op. cit.*, pp.20–21; Roy Clements, *Where love and
   justice meet* (Leicester: IVP, 1988), p.31
3. Genesis 1.26
4. Sanh. 10.5, cited in F. Cruseman, 'Human Solidarity and Ethnic Identity', in M.G. Brett, *Ethnicity and the Bible* (Leiden: E.J.
   Brill, 1996), p.66
5. Romans 3.23
6. Jonathan Glover, *Humanity: A moral history of the twentieth
   century* (London: Pimloco, 1999), p.310
7. Sacks, *op. cit.*, p.52
8. Sacks, *op. cit.*, p.53
9. Genesis 12.2–3
10. Church Dogmatics, III.4, Section 54.3, quoted in O.R.
    Johnston, *Nationhood: Towards a Christian Perspective* (Oxford:
    Latimer House, 1980), p.21
11. Romans 11.1, Acts 16.37, 22.25–28, Philippians 3.8
12. cf. Hays, *op. cit.*, p.193–99; Richard Bauckham, *The Climax of
    Prophecy* (Edinburgh: T & T Clark, 1993)
13. Revelation 5.9, 7.9, 10.11, 11.9, 13.7, 14.6, 17.15
14. Bauckham, *op. cit.*, p.336
15. For an interesting discussion on the balance between
    'nature' and 'creation' see Alister McGrath, *Nature*
    (Edinburgh: T&T Clark, 2001)
16. cf. David Koyzis, *Political Visions and Illusions* (Illinois: IVP,
    2003), pp.97–123
17. cf. N.T. Wright, *The New Testament and the People of God*
    (London: SPCK, 1992), pp.215–279
18. Wright, *op. cit.*, p.224–226
19. Deuteronomy 6.6–9

20. Leviticus 18.5, Deuteronomy 11.1, 4.40, 6.3, 6.18, 4.6–8
21. Nick Spencer, *Apolitical Animal?: A Biblical Perspective on Engaging with Politics in Britain today* (Cambridge: Jubilee Centre, 2003), B.G.B Logsdon, *Multipolarity and Covenant: Towards a Biblical Framework for Constitutional Safeguards* (Cambridge: Jubilee Centre, 1989)
22. Deuteronomy 17.16–20
23. Ethnicity is, of course, a complex phenomenon. The word derives from the Greek 'ethnos' meaning nation or people but can incorporate shared distinctive racial, religious, linguistic and cultural characteristics. Often used self-evidently, it is in fact as slippery as many corresponding taxonomic classifications.
24. Wright, *op. cit.*, pp.230–32
25.. Ezra 9.10–12
26. Nehemiah 10.28–32
27. Hays, *op. cit.*, p.79
28. Josephus, *Against Apion*, 2.210
29. cf. Wright, *op. cit.*, pp.159–161
30. John 4.1–42
31. Jeremy Ive and Julian Rivers, 'Nationality' in *Jubilee Manifesto: A framework, agenda and strategy for Christian Social Reform* (IVP, forthcoming)
32. Matthew 5.16
33. John 18.36
34. 1 Peter 2.9
35. Philippians 3.20
36. Hebrew 11.13–16
37. Revelation 3.12, 21.2,14, 22.14,19, etc.
38. 1 Corinthians 9.19–23
39. John Wolffe, *God and Greater Britain: Religion and National Life in Britain and Ireland, 1843–1945* (London and New York: Routledge, 1994), p. 250

Chapter 7

1. For a lengthy reader in political theology cf. (ed.) O & J.L. O'Donovan, *From Irenaeus to Grotius: A Sourcebook in Christian Political Thought* (Grand Rapids, MI: Eerdmans, 2000)

2. William Temple, *Christianity and the Social Order* (London: Shepheard Walwyn, 1976), p.40
3. Yasmin Alibhai-Brown, *Who do we think we are?* (London: Penguin, 2000), p.31
4. cf., for example, Deuteronomy 7.7–8, 9.6, etc.
5. Northern Iraq (1992), Somalia (1992), Bosnia-Herzegovina (1992–95), Haiti (1994), Rwanda (1994–95), Kosovo (1999), East Timor (1999)
6. *States*, p.54
7. *Rigged Rules and Double Standards: Trade, globalisation and the fight against poverty* (Oxford: Oxfam, 2002); *States*, p.55
8. *States*, p.60
9. cf. Nick Spencer, *The measure of all things: a biblical perspective on money and value in Britain today* (Cambridge: Jubilee Centre, 2003)
10. *Colour Line*, Asian Dub Foundation (Nation Records, 2000)
11. cf. Nick Spencer, *Where do we go from here?: A biblical perspective on roots and mobility in Britain today* (Cambridge: Jubilee Centre, 2002)
12. For the wide range of uses of Genesis 1–3, see A.E. Harvey, *By what authority?* (London: SCM Press, 2001)
13. http://www.optimumpopulation.org/
14. cf. Julian Rivers, *Multiculturalism* (Cambridge Papers, Vol. 10, No. 4, December 2001)
15. It is worth noting the impact of the concerted cultural efforts made during World War Two. See, Weight, *Patriots*, pp.21–118
16. www.clearproject.co.uk
17. www.praxis.org.uk
18. www.ecsr.org.uk
19. www.ctbi.org.uk/ccrj